HEALING
YOURSELF

HEALING YOURSELF

A Step-by-Step Program for Better Health Through Imagery

Martin L. Rossman, M.D.

An *Institute for the Advancement of Health* Book

The Institute for the Advancement of Health, the voluntary national organization in the new field of mind-body-health, seeks to further the scientific understanding of how mind-body interactions affect health and disease. Its publications are meant to inform both the interested public and health professionals, and do not represent an endorsement of any practitioner or modality.

First published in the United States of America in 1987 by the Walker Publishing Company, Inc.

Published simultaneously in Canada by Thomas Allen & Son Canada, Limited, Markham, Ontario.

Library of Congress Cataloging-in-Publication Data

Rossman, Martin L.
Healing yourself.

Includes index.
1. Imagery (Psychology)—Therapeutic use.
2. Self-care, Health. I. Title.
RC489.F35R67   1987   615.8'51   87-10515
ISBN 0-8027-0986-9

Printed in the United States of America

10 9 8 7 6 5

Text design by Manuela Paul

Table of Contents

Acknowledgments

Certain people have played especially important roles in the development of my understanding of imagery and healing. I am eternally indebted to Irving Oyle, D.O., who first showed me the healing power of thoughts and images by working wonders with patients in front of my skeptical eyes. Naomi Remen, M.D., has made major contributions to this book and my life as a teacher, colleague, guide, and friend. She reminds me without fail that life and healing are journeys of the soul. David Bresler, Ph.D., my partner in developing guided imagery training for health professionals, has taught me a great deal about both imagery and teaching, and has long encouraged me as both friend and colleague to write this book. Tom Yeomans, Ph.D., a master teacher and guide, has helped me to understand the healing process at the deepest personal levels I have been able to explore.

I want to especially thank Ken Pelletier, Ph.D., not just for taking the time from his busy schedule to write the introduction, but for his consistent and generous support of my work through the years.

Thanks to my editors, Harris Dienstfrey of the

Institute for the Advancement of Health and Richard Winslow of Walker and Company, for bringing this book to life and taking care to make it the best book it could be. Thanks, too, to Kathy Sullivan, my office manager, who has helped me with the manuscript in innumerable ways.

My love and deep gratitude to my parents, Manuel and Marion Rossman, and the rest of my family, who have always loved and supported me, and special thanks to my wife, Mie, for her patience, love, and understanding through our years together.

Finally, I want to thank my patients, who have shared their inner worlds with me, and who have had the courage to engage themselves with the challenge of healing.

Introduction

Beginning in the early 1950s, researchers and clinicians in Europe, Japan, China, and the United States began to explore systematically the role of imagery as an important factor in determining an individual's health or illness and, perhaps, life and death. During the past three decades, findings from several areas—basic stress research, biofeedback instrumentation, the clinical use of relaxation, and most recently, the emerging field of psychoneuroimmunology—have built an extensive body of knowledge indicating that psychological factors can and do significantly affect the physiology of the body.

At the present time, there are three convergent lines of inquiry that underscore the importance of mental imagery in mind-body interactions. First is the basic research in psychoneuroimmunology, which is the rather cumbersome term used to characterize the investigation of the interactions between the mind (psycho), the brain and central nervous system (neuro), and the body's biochemical resistance to disease and abnormal cell development (immunology). Since the early eighties, data from this discipline have brought new insights into the way psychological elements can contribute to allergies, to susceptibility to ailments ranging from colds to cancer, and perhaps to the mechanisms underlying AIDS and spontaneous remission. Also relevant in the domain of basic research has been the development of second generation imaging technologies such as PET (positron electron tomography) and NMR (nuclear magnetic resonance), which can picture brain activity with increasing specificity. Together these two developments unequivocally indicate the variety and subtlety of mind-body interactions. Medical technologies have begun to provide the basis for observing how and why imagery exerts its influence in healing.

A second line of inquiry is a growing body of clinical experimental research that serves as the bridge between basic research and its eventual widespread application in daily practice. A measure of the importance of this research is found in an article in the *Journal of the American Medical Association,* William H. Foege's "Public Health and Preventive Medicine" (October 25, 1985). That article pointed out that about two-thirds of the deaths in this country are *premature* "given our present medical knowledge" and that about two-thirds of the years of life lost before age 65 are "theoretically preventable given our current capabilities." Underlying this remarkable situation is our behavior, or lifestyle, which can exert a profound influence on health. Later on, the same article states, "In the coming decades, the most important determinants of health and longevity will be the personal choices made by each individual. This is both frightening, for those who wish to avoid such responsibility, and exciting for those who desire some control over their own destiny." In short, changes in behavior—outer and inner—can reduce the large number of premature deaths and illnesses and lead to better health and a longer life.

Clinical research has already demonstrated the impact of behavior upon disorders ranging from advanced heart disease to chronic pain. Behavioral approaches to illness give individuals the means to improve their health through their own efforts. Central to such approaches is the informed application of relaxation techniques and visual imagery, sensibly coordinated with appropriate medical and psychological care.

A third line of inquiry into the effects of imagery on health brings us directly to the basis of Dr. Martin Rossman's superb book—the day-to-day clinical applications and experience of skilled practitioners such as Dr. Rossman, who fuse insights from basic research and clinical-experimental studies with insight, compassion, and incisive clinical judgment into effective patient care. When I first met Dr. Rossman in 1974, during a conference at the UCLA School of Medicine, I was struck by his dedication to the healing profession, and in our collegial relationship and personal friendship since then, I have remained deeply impressed with the caring he exhibits to patients, colleagues, and friends. After more than fifteen years as a general practitioner, he has now distilled his insights concerning the healing role of imagery and the process of communicating with one's inner advisor into an accessible, practical, and effective book for both patients and practitioners.

What is unique about this book is that it teaches practical skills that are applicable to a wide range of disorders, and yet it is never glib or simplistic. An especially helpful feature of the book is that it addresses and suggests resolutions to the problems that sometimes arise as individuals begin using imagery as a form of mind–body communication. Dr. Rossman gives appropriate due to "resistance," not as an impediment, but as the voice of the loyal opposition that can offer an individual great insight into why he or she "needs" a disease or symptom. The book also shows how a patient can use the techniques of imagery to clarify choices that can undermine health, and then to rectify them, often with a profound, positive impact upon one's attitudes and physical being.

It is important to recognize that Dr. Rossman's use of imagery and his treatment of an inner advisor have a rich lineage stretching back thousands of years across many cultures. "Enlightenment" or "awakening" attained by inner guidance is a central element in ancient religious systems ranging from the Tibetan Buddhist *Abhidharma,* to Native American Indian beliefs, to the hierarchy of guardian angels in many western religions. Although these traditions may seem far removed from the daily practice of modern medicine, Dr. Rossman's book presents an eminently practical application of many of their most profound insights.

One of the greatest periods of western science was the eighteenth century period of the "Enlightenment." Significantly, this period arose from the fusion of inner and outer knowledge. Such a fusion characterizes this book, which can be a major step toward enlightenment and healing for anyone willing to engage it seriously.

Kenneth R. Pelletier, Ph.D.
Associate Clinical Professor
Department of Medicine
University of California
School of Medicine
San Francisco, California

Preface

This is not a pie-in-the-sky book.

While it's about imagining, it's extremely practical.

This book will teach you a step-by-step method of using your mind to help further your own healing. You will learn to use mental imagery to achieve deep physiologic relaxation, stimulate healing responses in your body, and create an inner dialogue that can help you better understand your health and what you can do to improve it. The method is one I have taught to thousands of patients and health professionals since 1972. It can be helpful, though not always curative, in 90 percent of the problems that people bring to a primary care doctor.

In the pages that follow, I will describe my introduction to the healing powers of imagery, present a model of how it may work, and share with you some of the healing I have witnessed in people who have learned to use this powerful tool. I will describe the nine imagery skills that I have found most helpful, and then provide scripts that will teach you each skill. I will also address the stumbling blocks and questions that most often arise when people begin to use imagery for healing.

"Healing" is sometimes treated like a dirty word in medicine. Some feel the term smacks of mysticism and quackery. Yet healing is a natural property of life. Healing happens because our integrity, at every level from the cellular to the psychological, is constantly challenged by life's changes, and we, like all living organisms, need to maintain a steady state in order to thrive. Without innate abilities to restore, replenish, and repair, life could not go on. In many ways, life itself is a continual process of healing, of moving toward balance and wholeness in the midst of change.

There are many ways you can help or hinder this natural process. The quality of food you eat can profoundly affect your ability to heal, as can the air you breathe, and drugs or medicines you take. Rest often supports healing, as does appropriate exercise. Your environment and social relationships also have important effects on your health, as do your thoughts, your feelings, and the way you use your mind.

This book is about the mental aspects of healing—the effects of your thoughts on your physical, emotional, and spiritual well-being. It will teach you specific ways to use your imagination and will to cooperate with your body's natural desire and ability to heal. It is designed for you whether you have a chronic or serious illness, or are primarily interested in health and wellness.

Before you begin, two words of caution. First, the self-healing techniques you will learn in this book may allow you to be more independent of medical care, but *they are not a substitute for it.* A good medical assessment is an important part of responsible self-care. If you have a symptom or illness that seems serious, or one that is persistent or recurrent, see your doctor for a diagnosis and recommendations for treatment. If you are unsure about your doctor's advice, seek a second and even a third opinion. You may also want to explore treatment options with qualified, ethical alternative health practitioners. If opinions conflict, a medical doctor educated in alternative health approaches may be best qualified to help you choose the best mode of treatment for you.

Using self-healing techniques without making a careful assessment of your condition can be dangerous and even life-threatening. I have known people who have needlessly died from curable illnesses because they would not consider conventional medical treatment. There is no inherent conflict between good medicine and self-care. Properly used, each complements the other.

When people seek my opinion about self-healing approaches for their illnesses, my first goal is to help them assess the risk thay may be taking by postponing medical treatment. I talk with their family doctors and appropriate specialists to determine whether they can safely explore alternatives for a six-week to three-month period. I ask the other doctors to monitor their progress during that time as a guard against self-deception. In most cases, they are happy to cooperate.

In some cases, the risk of delaying treatment precludes a safe trial of self-healing, and a medical or surgical intervention is necessary. Even then, self-healing techniques may help any treatment work more effectively, can help to speed healing, and can minimize adverse effects of treatments.

A second precaution applies if your symptoms or illness can be triggered by stress or emotional reactions. If so, you may bring on symptoms when you begin working with imagery. If this happens, you should feel encouraged—if imagery can provoke your symptoms, it can almost always be used to relieve them. If you have potentially dangerous symptoms, however, like anginal (heart) pains, or asthma, be sure to have medications at hand that can reliably alleviate them.

If your condition is really unstable and potentially dangerous, you might consider working first with a professional who can both guide you in your imagery and attend to appropriate medical precautions.

Most of the time, however, symptoms pose no immediate danger, and if you are not neglecting good medical care, you can safely experiment with imagery to see how effective you can be in healing yourself. With thoughtful use, imagery is a safe, inexpensive, and often effective addition to your healing effort, and the only experiment that will tell you if it will help you is the one you do yourself.

The skills I will teach you are the ones I have seen work most consistently in my general medical practice over the past fifteen years. In the pages that follow, you will meet some of the people (their identities disguised) I have been privileged to know who have used these methods to recover from their illnesses and others who have built rich lives in spite of illness. Their healing experiences are often physical, usually emotional, always attitudinal, and frequently spiritual. I hope their successes will inspire you to explore your own self-healing capabilities.

While there are many good books available that

mention or teach imagery skills for self-care (see Appendix B), they tend to focus either on the theoretical and research aspects of imagery, or on its use in particular symptoms or illnesses. In my practice and workshops I am often asked for a clear, simple guidebook to using imagery for self-healing across the broad spectrum of common health problems. This book is my attempt to share with you what I have learned. I hope it will be helpful to you.

M.L.R.
Mill Valley, California
June 1987

"Imagination is a good horse to carry you over the ground, not a magic carpet to take you away from the world of possibilities."

Robertson Davies, *The Manticore*

ONE

Faith Healing, Placebo Effects, and Imagery

When I was in my second year of practice, working in the county medical clinic, a middle-aged woman named Edna came in for a checkup. She was a likable, talkative person who said she was there because "the doctors worry me so and tell me I better keep an eye on my blood pressure." Her chart revealed that she had been diagnosed with a precancerous condition of the uterine cervix over two years previously, and the gynecologists she had seen wanted to take biopsies and remove the affected areas. Edna had turned this recommendation down four times, and each successive note by her gynecologic consultants was more frustrated and concerned in tone. There was mention of possible psychopathology and "irrational beliefs about healing."

When I asked Edna why she was unnecessarily risking her life, she smiled broadly and told me that "Jesus will heal me, and I don't need surgery." She said she prayed and talked to Jesus every day, and he promised he would heal her if she put her trust in him.

I asked her how she communicated with Jesus, and

1

she told me, "I see him when I pray, and he talks to me just like we're talking now." I again explained the medical concerns I and the other doctors had about her. Then I told her I had no doubt that Jesus could heal her if he wanted to, but wondered how long it would take. She was a bit surprised when I asked her if she would be willing to get in touch with him and ask him if he'd agree to heal her in the next six weeks.

She closed her eyes, and after a few minutes smiled and nodded her head. "Yes, he says he can and will heal me in six weeks." She agreed to have another pelvic exam and Pap smear at that time and also agreed to have a cone biopsy if the Pap smear was still abnormal. "But it won't be," she said, "I know that now." And she left, smiling more widely than ever. I felt good to have been able to get a commitment out of her to have a biopsy if her prayer proved ineffective.

Six weeks later she returned. Her cervix looked normal on examination. Three days later her Pap smear report came back—perfectly normal.

Edna's story certainly does not mean that you can forego Pap smears or that you must believe in Jesus. It does, however, point to the potent healing effects of faith and belief.

The Power of Positive Expectant Faith

I had, of course, like most physicians, witnessed the placebo effect on many occasions. It wasn't uncommon at the county hospital to give water injections to overly dramatic patients complaining of pain, while telling them it was powerful pain medication. Many times it relieved the pain as effectively as if it had been morphine. At the time, we thought such a response could tell us if the pain was "real" or not. As we'll see, the issue is not that simple.

I had also noticed with interest how many people began to feel better the instant they took the first dose of a medication known to take hours, days, or even weeks to begin working pharmacologically. Not to mention how many times people began to feel better as soon as I wrote their prescriptions!

No one knows exactly how these effects come about, but they are everyday occurrences in medicine. The placebo effect has been determined to be responsible for over half the action of some of our most powerful and trusted drugs and much of the action of any therapy—alternative or conventional, medical, surgical, or psychological.[1]

Belief can not only draw positive reactions from neutral substances, it can even cause people to react in opposition to the pharmacologic effects of a medication. A physician reported giving syrup of ipecac to two patients with severe nausea and vomiting. Ipecac is a very powerful emetic (it makes you vomit) and is usually given to people who have swallowed poisons in an effort to clear their stomachs. In this case, the patients were told that the ipecac was a very strong medicine that would soothe their stomachs and stop their vomiting—and it did![2]

The power of expectation and faith affects even surgical outcomes. In the 1950s there was a good deal of enthusiasm for an operation that was quite successful in

relieving chest pain (angina pectoris) and improving
heart function in men with blockage of their coronary
arteries. The operation involved making an incision
next to the breastbone and tying off a relatively superficial artery, which theoretically shunted more blood to
the arteries supplying the heart. Most of the patients
who underwent this procedure improved dramatically
with both relief of pain and improvement in heart
function. Then a controlled study was done on the
operation. A matched group of men with similar angina
were brought to the operating room, anesthetized, and a
surgical incision was made. These men, however, were
sewn up without anything else being touched. After
surgery, they experienced the same dramatic relief of
anginal pain and enjoyed the same improvement in
heart muscle functioning as the men who underwent the
real operation.[3]

To call a response "placebo" does not mean the
response isn't real. It simply means the results stem
from the belief of the patient in the therapy, rather than
from the therapy itself. *The important thing about the
placebo response is that it demonstrates beyond doubt that
thoughts can trigger the body's own self-healing abilities.*

Somehow, under certain conditions, our intentions, desires, and beliefs in recovery are translated into
physical healing. What are the conditions that allow this
to happen? If we can be "tricked" into healing, why
wouldn't we be able to do it on purpose? How can we
best use our minds and our wills to further the process
of healing? What are the "best" thoughts for healing?
These questions have motivated me since I first worked
with Edna and ultimately led to my involvement with
imagery.

My Introduction to Imagery

In 1972 I visited a doctor friend of mine who was working in an experimental health clinic in the seaside town of Bolinas, California. The founder and director of the clinic was a physician named Irving Oyle, who had retired to Bolinas from his general practice in New York. Dr. Oyle, who now lives and teaches in Eugene, Oregon, had at that time combined his interests in physics, parapsychology, psychology, and medicine into an informal clinical study of alternative healing methods. He was a masterful clinician who seemed almost to be able to talk his patients into getting well.

Instead of routinely prescribing medicines, Dr. Oyle would have his patients relax and visualize themselves healing, or have them imagine having a conversation with a wise figure who could tell them why they were sick and what they could do to get better.

At that time, I was studying and beginning to practice acupuncture in a neighboring town. Dr. Oyle was also researching acupuncture, and I began to visit the clinic frequently to compare notes. During my visits I became fascinated with the self-awareness and clinical improvement people seemed to be experiencing from working with his imagery techniques.

My interest in imagery remained rather superficial, however, until later that year when I heard a radiation oncologist, Dr. Carl Simonton, and his then wife, Stephanie Matthews-Simonton, a psychologist, present several cases of patients with untreatable cancers who seemed to have recovered with the use of a simple visualization technique. The technique consisted of relaxing and picturing their immune cells as numerous, aggressive, and powerful, destroying the cancer cells which were visualized as isolated, weak, and confused. The Simontons reported that people imagined the battle in many different ways—from knights on horseback routing their enemies to vicious dogs gobbling up chunks of meat. The anatomic accuracy of the image did not seem to matter as much as the enthusiasm and frequency of the practice. The Simontons have since gone on, together and independently, to expand their method into a comprehensive psychological program for dealing with cancer, but their initial work with imagery stirred a great deal of public and professional interest in the healing power of imagery. It certainly stimulated mine.

I began to work closely with Dr. Oyle for the next three years, seeing patients with him and immersing myself in the explosion of theoretical, experimental, and clinical information about mental effects on healing that surfaced in the early to mid-1970s. I had already studied Eastern psychologies and learned several forms of meditation while in medical school. Now I studied Jungian psychology, hypnosis, Gestalt therapy, Neurolinguistic Programming, and Psychosynthesis. I took courses like Silva Mind Control and Mind Dynamics. I learned about quantum physics, holography, and solipsism. I became more knowledgeable in fields ranging from neurophysiology to parapsychology, and found useful information about healing in all these sources. I also paid careful attention to the research that was emerging from the laboratories of people like Neal Miller, Ph.D., at Rockefeller University, Herbert Benson, M.D., at Harvard, and Elmer and Alyce Green, Ph.D., at the

Menninger Foundation. They and many others began to put a scientific foundation under the profuse flowering of psychophysiologic healing approaches.

My association with Dr. Oyle enabled me to meet many of the important pioneers in holistic medicine and exchange experiences and ideas with them. They all shared a great deal of enthusiasm about the human potential for self-healing, and imagery seemed always to play an important and often central role in their methods.

Most significantly, I watched my patients who were willing to try these "new" methods (many of which are thousands of years old). I saw how pleased they were to be able to relax, to relieve pain, to learn from their illnesses, and to be able to do something to help themselves. I was surprised on an almost daily basis at the kinds of problems that responded to imagery of one sort or another. Fifteen years later, I'm still frequently surprised.

Science and the Practice of Healing

There have been literally thousands of scientific studies demonstrating attitudinal, emotional, and behavioral effects on physiology and healing since my interest in this area began.[4] There remains, nevertheless, especially in the medical community, a resistance to the idea that people can do anything to influence their own healing. Skeptics claim that many of the methods I will teach you have not been scientifically proven, and they are right. In considering their role in healing, however, we need to take a closer look at the relationship between scientific proof and the clinical practice of medicine.

The institution of medicine bases much of its authority on the claim that it is a scientific discipline, and it rightly looks for scientific proof underlying claims of therapeutic effectiveness. While this is a noble goal, the fact is that the day-to-day practice of medicine includes very little that is scientifically well-proven and a good deal that is not. The "gold standard" of scientific proof is the double-blind controlled study. In such a study, neither patients receiving treatments nor the doctors administering treatments know what the patient is getting. The outcome is assessed by independent analysts who don't know whether patients received real or placebo treatments. These extreme measures to maintain secrecy are taken in order to separate the always-present placebo effect from the effect of the treatment being tested.

While double-blind studies are the most definitive, very few clinical studies are of this design. In fact, as recently as 1976, fewer than 5 percent of original research articles published in the *New England Journal of Medicine*, the *Journal of the American Medical Association*, and the *Lancet* were controlled matched studies of *any* kind. Only a fraction of that small percentage were double-blind. (5)

If doctors were to limit themselves to using only treatments that have been conclusively proven worthwhile through double-blind studies, doctors would prescribe very little treatment at all. Yet because our patients are suffering, we must often use our best judgment in suggesting other, less rigorously proven treatment. Ideally, we choose from remedies that have a long history of effectiveness and safety in clinical experience or, if no such option is available, from newer methods whose potential benefits outweigh their potential risks by a large enough margin. This conflict between necessity and certainty in treatment is so fundamental to medical practice that it is addressed on page one of *Harrison's Textbook of Internal Medicine,* one of the most widely used medical textbooks in print. Harrison says:

> In the practice of medicine the physician employs a discipline which seeks to utilize scientific methods and principles in the solution of its problems, but is one which, in the end, remains an art . . . in the sense that the practicing physician can never be content with the sole aim of clarifying the laws of nature; he cannot proceed in his labors with the cool detachment of the scientist whose aim is the winning of truth, and who, theoretically, is uninterested in the practical outcome of his work. The practicing physician must never forget that his primary and traditional objectives are utilitarian—the prevention and cure of disease and the relief of suffering, whether of body or mind.

Faced with illness, distress, and uncertainty, the informed patient and the practicing physician must often consider options that may not be rigorously proven as they attempt to formulate a sensible plan for treatment and self-care.

Even simple clinical research on humans is difficult

because of the many influences on outcome that cannot
be controlled. Add to this the difficulty of trying to
determine what an individual is really thinking, and we
are faced with the very real possibility that it may *never*
be possible to conclusively prove or disprove the theory
that thoughts can ameliorate or cure disease.

Another factor that makes imagery particularly
difficult to quantify scientifically is that it often is involved in healing in ways that might best be termed
nonlinear. Healing may not be a simple matter of imagining a problem disappearing and having it disappear.
Imagery may help a patient become aware of how his or
her symptoms develop, and lead to changes in attitude
or behavior that then lead to recovery. Let me share an
illustrative case with you from my practice.

Alexandra was thirty years old, active and successful, but worried. She had developed a number of lumps
in her breast. Several eminent physicians had diagnosed
them as benign nodules but she worried that they were
precancerous, and wanted to know if she could do
anything to make them go away.

Alexandra was intensely involved in every aspect
of her life. She worked long hours, traveled frequently
in her work, and kept a busy social schedule as well. She
often felt tense and tired, and wanted less stress in her
life, though she saw that as a problem separate from her
breast lumps.

As part of our consultation, I asked her to relax and
let an image of the lumps come to mind. She imagined
them as rocks in a stream, and was upset to see they
were partially obstructing its flow. As she looked more
closely, however, her perception of the rocks changed
dramatically. She noticed that they were very smooth,

shiny, and lustrous, and looked more like pearls than rocks. Alexandra immediately understood that, like pearls in an oyster, these lumps had formed in response to irritation and represented an attempt to protect her from further harm.

When I asked her what would need to happen for the pearls to be able to dissolve, she sensed a need to "remove the source of irritation." She made changes in her scheduling, her traveling, and her diet, and the lumps in her breast disappeared within a few months.

By paying attention to her problem in this way, Alexandra not only learned a valuable lesson in stress management, she personally experienced the wisdom of her body and mind working together to maintain a healthy equilibrium. Her symptoms got her attention, and her imagery allowed her to understand both the meaning of her symptoms and what she needed to do to allow healing to proceed. In her case, the imagery did not dissolve her lumps directly, but showed her what she could do to allow that to happen.

How would you quantify the effect that imagery had in Alexandra's recovery? For science, that is the question, and a difficult one indeed. Fortunately, you don't need to wait until this issue is decided scientifically to see whether or not this approach will be of help to you. As long as you heed the precautions I described in the Foreword, imagery is quite safe and offers potential benefits that far outweigh its risks.

You are your own research laboratory and granting authority for experimenting with self-healing. You have the need, the opportunity, and the right to explore this method for yourself. You would have to do this in any case, since no treatment works for everyone. Even if these techniques had been irrefutably proven to work 90 percent of the time, you would still have to find out if they work for you.

In the following chapters, you, like Alexandra, will learn to use your imagination to better understand your health and to influence it for the better. First, let's take a closer look at the nature of imagery, its known effects on physiology, and the possible mechanisms of its ability to affect body and mind.

NOTES

1) Evans, Frederick J. (1985), "Expectations and the Placebo Response." In *Placebo: Clinical Phenomena and New Insights,* ed. L. White, B. Tursky, and G. E. Schwartz. New York: Guilford Press.

2) Wolf, S. (1950), "Effects of suggestion and conditioning on the actions of chemical agents in human subjects—the psychopharmacology of placebos." *Journal of Clinical Investigation,* 29:100–109.

3) Beecher, H. K. (1961), "Surgery as placebo." *Journal of the American Medical Association,* 176:1102–1107. Both this and the previous study are described along with many others in the classic *Persuasion and Healing,* Jerome Frank, M.D., Schocken Books, 1963, New York.

4) Some idea of the scope of this literature can be gained from *Mind and Immunity,* and *Psychological and Behavioral Treatments for Disorders of the Heart and Blood Vessels,* the first two volumes in a series of publications by the Institute for the Advancement of Health. They review over thirteen hundred scientific studies on the effects of the mind on immunity and over nine hundred studies on psychological and behavioral treatments for cardiovascular disorders. Information on this series and the excellent journal of the Institute, *Ad-*

vances, can be obtained by writing the Institute at 16 East Fifty-Third Street, New York, N.Y., 10022.

5) Fletcher, R. H., and Fletcher, S. W. (1979), "Clinical research in general medical journals: a 30-year perspective." *New England Journal of Medicine,* 301:180–183.

TWO

What Is Imagery, and How Does it Work?

Imagery is a flow of thoughts you can see, hear, feel, smell, or taste. An image is an inner representation of your experience or your fantasies—a way your mind codes, stores, and expresses information. Imagery is the currency of dreams and daydreams; memories and reminiscence; plans, projections, and possibilities. It is the language of the arts, the emotions, and most important, of the deeper self.

Imagery is a window on your inner world; a way of viewing your own ideas, feelings, and interpretations. But it is more than a mere window—it is a means of transformation and liberation from distortions in this realm that may unconsciously direct your life and shape your health.

Imagination, in this sense, is not sufficiently valued in our culture. The imaginary is equated with the fanciful, the unreal, and the impractical. In school we are taught the three R's while creativity, uniqueness, and interpersonal skills are either barely tolerated or frankly discouraged. As adults, we are usually paid to perform tasks, not to think creatively. The premium is on the practical, the useful, the real, as it should be—but imagination nurtures human reality as a river brings life to a desert.

Without imagination, humanity would be long extinct. It took imagination—the ability to conceive of new possibilities—to make fire, create weapons, and cultivate crops; to construct buildings, invent cars, airplanes, space shuttles, television, and computers.

Paradoxically, our collective imagination, which has allowed us to overcome so many natural threats, has been instrumental in creating the major survival problems we face on earth today—pollution, exhaustion of natural resources, and the threat of nuclear annihilation. Yet imagination, teamed with will, remains our best hope for overcoming these same problems.

Imagery and Physiologic Change

Imagery in healing is probably best known for its direct effects on physiology. Through imagery, you can stimulate changes in many body functions usually considered inaccessible to conscious influence.

A simple example: Touch your finger to your nose. How did you do that? You may be surprised to learn that nobody knows.

A neuroanatomist can tell us the area of the brain where the first nerve impulses fire to begin that movement. We can also trace the chain of nerves that conduct impulses from the brain to the appropriate muscles. But *no one* knows how you go from thinking about touching your nose to firing the first cell in that chain. You just decide to do it and you do it, without having to worry about the details.

Now make yourself salivate.

You probably didn't find that as easy, and may not have been able to do it at all. That's because salivation is not usually under our conscious control. It is controlled by a different part of the nervous system than the one that governs movement. While the central nervous system governs voluntary movement, the autonomic nervous system regulates salivation and other physiologic functions that normally operate without conscious control. The autonomic nervous system doesn't readily respond to ordinary thoughts like "salivate." But it does respond to imagery.

Relax for a moment and imagine you are holding a juicy yellow lemon. Feel its coolness, its texture, and weight in your hand. Imagine cutting it in half and squeezing the juice of one half into a glass. Perhaps some pulp and a seed or two drop into the glass. Imagine raising the glass to your lips and taking a good mouthful of the tart juice. Swish it around in your mouth, taste its sourness, and swallow.

Now did you salivate? Did you pucker your lips or make a sour face when you imagined that? If you did, that's because your autonomic nervous system responded to your imaginary lemon juice.

You probably don't spend much time thinking about drinking lemon juice, but what you do habitually think about may have important effects on your body through a similar mechanism. If your mind is full of thoughts of danger, your nervous system will prepare you to meet that danger by initiating the stress response, a high level of arousal and tension. If you imagine peaceful, relaxing scenes instead, it sends out an "all-clear" signal, and your body relaxes.

Research in biofeedback, hypnosis, and meditative states has demonstrated a remarkable range of human self-regulatory capacities. Focused imagery in a relaxed state of mind seems to be the common factor among these approaches.

Imagery of various types has been shown to affect heart rate, blood pressure, respiratory patterns, oxygen consumption, carbon dioxide elimination, brain wave rhythms and patterns, electrical characteristics of the skin, local blood flow and temperature, gastrointestinal motility and secretions, sexual arousal, levels of various hormones and neurotransmitters in the blood, and immune system function.[1] But the healing potentials of imagery go far beyond simple effects on physiology.

Imagery in the Larger Context of Healing

Recovering from a serious or chronic illness may well demand more from you than simple imagery techniques. It may also require changes in your lifestyle, your attitudes, your relationships, or your emotional state. Imagery can be an effective tool for helping you see what changes need to be made, and how you can go about making them.

Imagery is the interface language between body and mind. It can help you understand the needs that may be represented by an illness and can help you develop healthy ways to meet those needs. Let me give you another example from my practice. Jeffrey was a successful middle manager in his thirties who had recurrent peptic ulcers for many years. In our work together he learned to relax and use simple visualization to give himself temporary relief from his stomach pain. He pictured the pain as a fire in his stomach and would then imagine an ice-cold mountain stream extinguishing the fire and cooling the scorched area beneath it. He was surprised and pleased to find that relaxing and imagining this process for a few minutes would relieve his pain for several hours to a day at a time, and he used it successfully for about two weeks. Then it stopped working. His pain grew worse in spite of his visualizations, and he began to despair. In our next session I suggested he focus once more on the pain and allow an image to arise that might help him understand why the pain had returned. He soon became aware of an image of a hand pinching the inside of his stomach.

At my suggestion, he mentally asked the hand if it would tell him why it was pinching him, and it changed into an arm shaking a clenched fist. He asked the arm why it was angry, and it replied, "Because there's a part of you locked away where no one can see it, and it's getting badly hurt." I asked him to form an image of the part that was locked away, and he saw a transparent sack that contained a "chaotic whirling of things inside—nothing is clear, everything is zooming around, bumping into everything else." All he could make out were colors and shapes and a sense of discomfort. After observing them for a while, he quietly said, "My heart is in there, and it's getting bumped and bruised by all these things."

I asked Jeffrey to imagine opening the bag, but as he began he became afraid and said there was too much pain there to let out all at once. I asked him to let just one thing out of the bag and let an image form for it. He imagined his father's face and recalled a number of painful childhood interactions with his father, who was quite emotionally abusive. Over a series of sessions, he began to come to terms with the feelings he had locked away about this and started to feel much better emotionally and physically. In this way, he not only obtained relief from his ulcer pain, he learned a method to better express and respond to his own emotional needs.

Using imagery in this way can allow illness to become a teacher of wellness. Symptoms and illnesses indicate that something is out of balance, something needs to be adjusted, adapted to, or changed. Imagery can allow you to understand more about your illness and respond to its message in the healthiest imaginable way.

How Does Imagery Work?

The ultimate mechanisms of imagery are still a mystery. In the last twenty years, however, we have learned that imagery is a natural language of a major part of our nervous system. Critical to this understanding is the Nobel-prize-winning work of Dr. Roger Sperry and his collaborators at the University of Chicago and later at the California Institute of Technology. They have shown that the two sides of the human brain think in very different ways and are simultaneously capable of independent thought. In a real sense, we each have two brains. One thinks as we are accustomed to thinking, with words and logic. The other, however, thinks in terms of images and feelings.

In most people, the left brain is primarily responsible for speaking, writing, and understanding language; it thinks logically and analytically, and identifies itself by the name of the person to whom it belongs. The right brain, in contrast, thinks in pictures, sounds, spatial relationships, and feelings. It is relatively silent, though highly intelligent. The left brain analyzes, taking things apart, while the right brain synthesizes, putting pieces together. The left is a better logical thinker, the right is more attuned to emotions. The left is most concerned with the outer world of culture, agreements, business, and time, while the right is more concerned with the inner world of perception, physiology, form, and emotion.

The essential difference between the two brains is in the way each processes information. The left brain processes information sequentially, while the right brain processes it simultaneously. Imagine a train coming around a curve in the track. An observer is positioned on the ground, on the outside of the curve, and he observes the train to be a succession of separate though connected cars passing him one at a time. He can see just a little bit of the cars ahead of and behind the one he is watching. This observer has a "left-brain" view of the train.

The "right-brain" observer would be in a balloon several hundred feet above the tracks. From here he could not only see the whole train, but also the track on which it was traveling, the countryside through which it was passing, the town it had just left, and the town to which it was headed.

This ability of the right hemisphere to grasp the larger context of events is one of the specialized functions that make it invaluable to us in healing. The imagery it produces often lets you see the "big picture" and experience the way an illness is related to events and feelings you might not have considered important. You can see not only the single piece, but the way it's connected to the whole. This change of perspective may allow you to put ideas together in new ways to produce new solutions to old problems. A right-brain point of view may reveal the opportunity hidden in what seems to be a problem.

The right brain has a special relationship not only to imagery but to emotions. This is another of the major strengths it brings to the healing adventure. Many studies have shown that the right brain is specialized to recognize emotion in facial expressions, body language, speech, and even music. This is critical to healing because emotions are not only psychological but physical states that are at the root of a great deal of illness and disease. Rudolph Virchow, a nineteenth-century physician and founding father of the science of pathology, remarked that "Much illness is unhappiness sailing under a physiologic flag." Studies in England and the United States have found that from 50 to 75 percent of all problems presenting to a primary care clinic are emotional, social, or familial in origin, though they are being expressed by pain or illness.[2]

Emotions themselves are, of course, not unhealthy. On the contrary, they are a normal response to certain life events. Failure to acknowledge and express important emotions, however, is an important factor in illness, and one that is widespread in our society. In many ways we are emotional illiterates, lacking clear guidelines and traditions for expressing emotions in healthy

ways. It is difficult to know what to do with distressing
emotions such as grief, fear, and anger, so we cope as
best we can. We may unconsciously build layer upon
layer of inner defenses to protect us from feeling unpleasant feelings. But strong emotion has a way of
finding routes of expression. If not recognized and dealt
with for what it is, it may manifest as pain or illness.

Social and family relationships to some extent depend on our ability to process emotions internally. We
don't need to express every emotion we feel. But
strong, persistent emotions need to be expressed or
resolved, as their chronic denial may lead to physiologic
imbalance and disease. The story of Alice is one example of how holding back feelings can manifest as pain,
and how expressing them appropriately can lead to
relief.

Alice was a woman in her forties who had recently
undergone surgery and radiation to treat a breast cancer
discovered several months earlier. She was an intelligent, composed woman who felt that imagery and
visualization had already been enormously beneficial to
her in tolerating her treatment and recovering from her
cancer. She continued, however, to be bothered by a
persistent pain between her shoulder blades. Repeated
examinations and X-rays by her cancer specialists had
failed to identify any physical cause of her pain. She
wanted to understand why it was there, and what she
needed to do for it to go away.

We decided to use an imagery technique you will
learn later in this book: a talk with an imaginary wisdom figure called an inner advisor. Alice relaxed and
imagined herself on a beautiful beach at the base of a
high cliff. She asked for an image of her inner advisor

and saw a man who looked like Merlin the Magician, tending a fire. After greeting him, she asked him about her back pain.

After a few seconds of silence, she broke into tears. She told me her advisor said she needed to ask for help, and that's what brought on the tears. She had been strong and courageous throughout the entire cancer ordeal, calming and reassuring to her husband and family. She always went for checkups and treatments alone, though it frightened her, because she felt her husband and kids would be frightened if she asked them for help or company. Though she was often aware of her own doubts, fears, and concerns about her illness and its treatment, she had never allowed herself to express them in an attempt to spare her loved ones from the anxiety it might produce.

Alice told her inner advisor her concerns about her family being scared if she asked for help. Her advisor answered, "They are already scared. They will feel better if they are included in your trials and have an opportunity to be supportive and show their love for you." She realized at once that this was true. She imagined asking her husband John for help. She laughed, as in her mind's eye she saw him taking out his appointment book and thumbing through it. She asked him (still in imagery), "Do you have time?" and he looked at her over his half-glasses and said, "We'll make time." When she came out of the imagery her pain was substantially relieved, with "just enough left to remind me that I actually need to talk with John about this in real life."

Like Alice, we all may hold back emotions because of conflicts between our thoughts and feelings. This inner division has been recognized in the oldest stories of humanity. That it may on one level represent a disagreement between the two hemispheres is a new, potentially helpful way to understand this situation. As Dr. Joseph Bogen, of the California Institute of Technology, the neurosurgeon who helped reveal the dual nature of the hemispheres, has said, "Having two brains has allowed man to be the most creative animal on earth, since we have two chances to solve any given problem. At the same time it creates an unprecedented opportunity for inner conflict."

When there is inner conflict, the body is the battleground. It may pay dearly for prolonged, serious struggle. Bringing the conflicting sides, whether sides of the brain or sides of the argument, to the bargaining table may be the beginning of healing. The goal, after all, is not to become a "left-brain" or "right-brain" person, but a "whole-brain" person.

In any successful arbitration, both sides must have the opportunity to express themselves, to state their grievances, their desires, their needs, and what they can offer in the interest of peace. If they speak different languages, there must be an impartial translator willing to listen and speak for both sides, or the two must attempt to learn each other's languages. This is why imagery is important—it is a major language of the right brain.

Most of us understand and use left-brain language and logic every day. We are relatively familiar with our conscious needs and desires. Imagery gives the silent right brain a chance to bring its needs to light and to contribute its special qualities to the healing process.

Frankly, calling verbal or logical thinking "left-brained," and symbolic, imaginal thinking "right-brained" is an oversimplification, but it is a useful model for thinking about some uses of imagery. Imagery allows you to communicate with your own silent mind in its native tongue. Imagery is a rich, symbolic, and highly personal language, and the more time you spend observing and interacting with your own image-making brain, the more quickly and effectively you will use it to improve your health.

If you are ill, you have undoubtedly thought long and hard about why you fell ill and what you need to do to get better. If your illness is chronic, or severe, you have probably consulted many doctors, whose highly educated, logical analyses may have led to a diagnosis. Yet the diagnosis may not have led to a cure, or even relief. If good "left-brained" thinking has come to nought, why not get a "second opinion" from your other brain? After all, who is likely to know more about your body, your feelings, and your life?

What Kinds of Illnesses Can Be Treated With Imagery?

While preliminary studies have demonstrated that imagery can be an effective part of treatment in a wide variety of illnesses, I am reluctant to offer a list of "diseases that can be treated with imagery." Imagery can be helpful in so many ways that it is more accurate to think of it as a way of treating *people* than a way of treating illnesses.

Imagery can help you whether you have simple tension headaches or a life-threatening disease. Through imagery, you can learn to relax and be more comfortable in any situation, whether you are ill or well. You may be able to reduce, modify, or eliminate pain. You can use imagery to help you see if your lifestyle habits have contributed to your illness and to see what changes you can make to support your recovery. Imagery can help you tap inner strengths and find hope, courage, patience, perseverance, love, and other qualities that can help you cope with, transcend, or recover from almost any illness.

There are, of course, certain symptoms and illnesses that seem to be more readily responsive to imagery than others. Conditions that are caused by or aggravated by stress often respond very well to imagery techniques. These include such common problems as headaches, neck pain, back pain, "nervous stomach," spastic colon, allergies, palpitations, dizziness, fatigue, and anxiety. Other major health problems including heart disease, cancer, arthritis, and neurological illnesses are often complicated by or themselves cause stress, anxiety, and depression. The emotional aspects of any illness can often be helped through imagery, and relieving the emotional distress may in turn encourage physical healing.

I must repeat that good medical care for the serious problems mentioned above is essential and perfectly compatible with imagery. If you choose to have therapeutic treatments of any kind, acknowledge them as your allies in healing and include them in your imagery. If you are taking an antibiotic or chemotherapy, imagine the medicines coursing through your tissues, finding and eliminating the bacteria or tumor cells you are fighting. If you have surgery, imagine the operation going smoothly and successfully, and your recovery being rapid and complete. There is good evidence that this type of pre-operative preparation reduces recovery time and complications from surgery.[3]

Now that we've considered what imagery can do and how it might work, let's begin your personal exploration of the imagery process.

NOTES

1) A very good review of this literature is found in "Imagery, physiology, and psychosomatic illness," Sheikh, A., and Kunzendorf, R. G. (1984). In *International Review of Mental Imagery*, Vol. 1, ed. Sheikh, A. New York: Human Sciences Press.

2) Rosen, G., Kleinman, A., and Katon, W. (1982), "Somatization in family practice: a biopsychosocial approach". *Journal of Family Practice*, 14:3, 493–502.

Stoeckle, J. D., Zola, I. K., and Davidson, G. E. (1964), "The quantity and significance of psychological distress in medical patients." *Journal of Chronic Disease*, 17:959.

3) An excellent review of psychological factors in surgical outcome is found in "Behavioral Anesthesia," by Henry L. Bennett, Ph.D., in *Advances*, 2:4, Fall, 1985.

Pickett, C., and Clum, G. A. (1982), "Comparative treatment strategies and their interaction with locus of control in the reduction of postsurgical pain and anxiety." *Journal of Consulting and Clinical Psychology*, 50:3, 439–441,

THREE

A First Imagery Exploration

As a first step in working with imagery, I'd like to suggest that you begin a journal or notebook to record and monitor your experiences and progress. Consider this journal a diary of your personal experience with healing. Record your imagery experiences, your thoughts, feelings, questions, and changes in health status as you work. Use it to keep a record of your moods, your stress levels, your symptoms, diet, and activity level. Write in it, draw in it, paste newspaper articles or magazine pictures in it, and include anything else that has meaning for you in your healing work. This is your record—keep it in any form that will be most useful to you.

You will find this journal valuable in many ways as you become more aware of the many factors that influence your healing. Reviewing your journal from time to time will help you see the process as it unfolds, remind you of lessons already learned, and help you spot recurring patterns that may deserve more exploration.

Now let us begin to explore your imagery. One of the most common misunderstandings about imagery is that it requires you to be able to visualize. While imagery certainly includes what you see in your mind's eye, it also consists of what you hear in your inner ear, sensations and emotions that you feel inside, and even what you smell and taste in your imagination. Some people imagine in vivid visual images with color, sound, smell, and sensation, while others may experience sounds, songs, or thoughts in their heads without any pictures. Some will be more aware of senses or feelings that guide them and let them know when they are close to something meaningful. It doesn't really matter how you imagine—just that you learn to recognize and work with your own imagery. Your purpose is not to get pretty pictures—your purpose is to pay attention to what your body/mind is trying to tell you. Imagery is a vehicle to this understanding, which may come through inner pictures, words, thoughts, sensations, or feelings.

A simple script follows that will allow you to explore what imagery is like for you in different senses. It is a sampler that will allow you to experience how you use imagery most naturally. As you go through it, notice the different ways you imagine and which ways are easiest for you. There are no "right" or "wrong" images to have. Your task is merely to focus on what is being suggested and notice what images develop for you. Be an observer as well as a participant in the process.

How To Use the Imagery Scripts

There are a number of ways to use the scripts in this book. You may want to read through each exercise slowly, either mentally or aloud, pausing after each suggestion to experience your imagery. This first script is designed to be used this way, but the scripts that follow work much better if they are read to you, or tape-recorded. This will allow you to close your eyes, focus more easily inside, and immerse yourself in your inner experience.

You can tape-record the scripts yourself, speaking in a relaxed voice, pausing where indicated by ". . . ," and leaving enough time after each suggestion for the inner experience to unfold. If you have difficulty recording, or if your own voice is not soothing to you, you may have a friend with a calming manner and voice who will read or record the scripts for you.

If you record your own tapes, do a "sound check" early in the recording process. Record a few lines of the script, then stop and replay the tape to check for recording quality. It's frustrating to record a twenty-five minute tape and find you were too far away from the microphone, or that the "pause" button was on, or that the noise from an inexpensive recorder has drowned out your voice. Once you have acceptable sound quality, take a couple of deep breaths, relax, and begin to record.

You can also order audiotapes I have recorded of all the scripts in this book. These studio-recorded tapes usually have better sound quality than you can produce at home, and the phrasing, pacing, and voice modulation on them is the result of many years of practice and research.

However you decide to use the scripts, begin by selecting a quiet and private location where you won't be interrupted for about twenty to thirty minutes. Tell anyone who needs to know not to disturb you during this time except for a true emergency. Take the phone off the hook or turn on the answering machine. Loosen any clothing or jewelry that is tight or restrictive. Get in a comfortable position, either lying down or sitting, and remember that you can move or shift positions any time to become even more comfortable.

SCRIPT:

Exploring Your Imagery Abilities

Begin by getting comfortable where you are . . . let yourself breathe easily and comfortably . . . take a couple of slow, deep breaths and let the out breath be a real "letting go" kind of breath . . . just begin to let go of any unnecessary tension or discomfort . . . as you relax allow your eyes to close and begin to focus inside. . . .

As I ask you to imagine a variety of things, allow yourself to observe what happens for you . . . remember, there is no right or wrong way to imagine these things . . . just notice what it's like for you . . . that's your only responsibility now . . . noticing what it's like. . . .

Imagine a triangle in your mind's eye . . . any type of triangle will do . . . you may imagine you see it on a screen, like a movie or television screen, or you may imagine it in your mind . . . just notice which is easier for you . . . notice what type of triangle you see . . . perhaps there is more than one . . . notice if the image is steady and vivid, or if it comes and goes, or changes as you watch it . . . remember, it doesn't really matter how you imagine it . . . just stay relaxed and observe what is happening. . . .

If you'd like the image to be clearer or more vivid, imagine you have a set of controls like you do on your TV set, and experiment with them until the image is the way you want it . . . or just take a couple of deep breaths, and relax more deeply as you let them go, letting the image become clearer as you do . . . notice how these techniques work for you. . . .

Now let the image go . . . and let a square form in your mind's eye or on your mental screen . . . any kind of square is fine . . . just notice what it's like as you continue to observe it . . . now let that image fade and imagine a circle . . . notice how big or small it is, and how round . . . let the circle be yellow . . . a bright yellow circle . . . notice if it helps to think of the sun or a yellow lemon . . . let the yellow fade and imagine the circle is red . . . like an apple or something red that's familiar to you . . . now let that go and imagine the circle is blue . . . like the sky or the ocean . . . let the circle become three-dimensional and form a sphere . . . and let the sphere begin to rotate slowly . . . see it rotating and let it become a globe, spinning in space, as if you were looking back at the earth from outer space. . . .

Now come back to earth . . . imagine you are in the country, and it's wintertime . . . you are walking through the freshly fallen snow and can hear and feel it crunch beneath your boots . . . the air is cold and crisp, and you can see your breath as you exhale . . . in the distance a church bell is pealing . . . and somewhere a radio is playing "Jingle Bells" . . . notice what that sounds like. . . .

Now let that image fade and imagine instead you are on a beautiful warm tropical beach . . . the sky is blue, and the sun is bright and warm on your skin . . . the sand is warm beneath your feet . . . the ocean is vast, and the waves roll to the shore one after the other in a timeless, tireless rhythm . . . you can hear the sound of the waves breaking, advancing, and retreating on the sand . . . imagine that you walk down toward the water, feeling the sand becoming hotter underneath your feet . . . you may begin to walk a little more quickly as it becomes hotter and hotter . . . as you reach the waterline where the water has washed and cooled the sand you feel the relief of the cool wetness on the soles of your feet . . . as you walk a little way into the cool swirling water, it washes around your ankles, and as it retreats, it draws away some of the sand beneath your feet . . . the movement of the sand and water feels good beneath you. . . .

Now let that image go . . . and imagine you are in a room from your childhood—a room where you had some very good experiences . . . notice where you are . . . and what you see there . . . notice what sounds you hear there . . . and perhaps an odor or aroma that's special to that place . . . notice how it feels to be there. . . .

Let that image go . . . and imagine the aroma of fresh-ground coffee . . . now imagine there's a plate of your favorite food in front of you, beautifully prepared from the freshest ingredients . . . you lean over and inhale the aroma . . . then taste it . . . notice what it's like as you taste it, chew it . . . and swallow. . . .

Let that go . . . and imagine you are walking along a path in the forest . . . it's a beautiful day . . . and you meet someone friendly on the path . . . you

stop to have a brief conversation with this person . . .
notice who you meet and what you talk about . . .
notice how you communicate with one another. . . .

If there are any loose ends, or if you want to
continue this talk, arrange with the imaginary person
to meet again at a later time. . . .

Now let that go . . . and recall some time you felt
very much at peace with yourself . . . a time when you
felt very peaceful, very centered, and calm . . . imagine
it as if it were happening right now . . . notice where
you are . . . and who you're with . . . what you're
doing . . . notice your posture . . . and your face . . .
your voice . . . especially notice the feelings of peacefulness and centeredness in you . . . notice where you
feel these qualities, and let them be there . . . let them
begin to grow in you . . . let them amplify and expand, filling your whole body with feelings of peacefulness and calm . . . let the feelings overflow your
body to fill the space around you . . . so that all of you
is bathed in this peacefulness. . . .

Now slowly let yourself begin to become aware of
the room . . . and let yourself come awake and alert,
bringing back with you any feelings of peacefulness
you may have experienced . . . remember what was of
interest or importance to you, and take some time to
write about it. . . .

Evaluating Your Experience

As you write about your experience, you may want
to consider the following questions: Did you experience
any of the images as pictures? Sounds? Smells? Tastes?

Feelings? Which images came easily? Which were more difficult, and were there any you weren't able to imagine at all? Were you surprised by any particular images or your reactions to them?

Did you experience heat, cold, or other sensations at any time? If you did, you've already begun to influence your body through your imagery. If not, you may want to experiment with your own images until you can imagine these sensations.

Were you able to make your images clearer by adjusting imaginary controls? Or by relaxing more?

Did anything of special interest or importance happen? Did you have emotional reactions to any of the images? Could you develop a sense of peacefulness in the last part of the exercise? If not, work with that part of the script again until you can recall or imagine yourself feeling peaceful. When this happens, you have taken an important step in creating a positive emotional state for yourself—by choice. If you were able to notice changes in sensation or mood from this first imagery exploration, it's an indication that your body is particularly responsive to your imagery, and you are an excellent candidate for using imagery to improve your health. If you didn't notice any change, however, don't despair. Like any skill, imagery takes time to learn, and you may first need to learn to relax your body and quiet your mind in order to notice results.

Whether you have already noticed changes or not, learning to relax deeply and reliably will assist your movement toward better health in many ways. The next chapter will tell you how and teach you a simple method for creating a pleasant state of mental and physical relaxation.

FOUR

Imagery, Stress, and Relaxation

The most common form of imagery that affects our health is *worry*. It is imagination that allows us to react not only to current stressors, but to anticipated dangers in the future and remembered grief from the past. Uncontrolled imagination gives humans the unique ability to compress a lifetime of stress into every passing moment.

Worry is an excellent example of the psychophysiologic power of imagery. When you worry you focus on thoughts of danger and disaster, which may or may not come to pass. As you do this, your body becomes tense and aroused, anticipating a threat or challenge. The "fight or flight" response is activated, initiating a chain of physiologic changes that ready you for intense physical activity. Your body is on alert and prepared for the worst.

Yet imagined threats may never materialize, and, worse, may never go away. If you are a habitual worrier, one worry replaces another, and the cycle is never resolved. You don't release your pent-up energy, don't take the opportunity to relax, and your system can't rebuild its depleted reserves. Eventually, you become exhausted, "stressed-out," "burned-out," sick and tired. The only threats have been the thoughts themselves, though your responses and their physiologic toll have been quite real.

If the toll has become too great, you can help yourself by becoming skilled in the use of your imagination. You can learn to become aware of and change habitual, unconscious thought patterns that lead to tension and depression. It takes some work, but it can be done, and imagery is a key to doing it. The first imagery skill you need to learn is how to STOP doing the troublesome imagery you are already doing and focus on thoughts that let you RELAX. In this chapter you will learn specific techniques that will help you learn to do just that.

Learning to relax is fundamental to self-healing and a prerequisite for using imagery effectively. Relaxation is a first exercise in focusing and concentrating your mind on the process of healing. In addition, deep physiologic relaxation has health benefits of its own. It allows your body to channel its energy into repair and restoration and provides respite from habitual patterns of tension. Let me share two brief cases from my practice that illustrate the potential benefits of simple relaxation.

Ed was a middle-aged man who came to me ten years ago complaining of recurrent sinus infections, constant hay fever, and severe daily headaches above and behind his eyes. Regular doses of aspirin, decongestants, and antihistamines were of minimal help. Conventional allergy testing showed he was sensitive to many pollens and airborne chemicals. He was much worse on smoggy days and when the pollen count was high. Years of allergy shots had helped somewhat but had lost their effectiveness in the year preceding his visit to me. Ed was a busy, caring person, deeply involved with his family, his church, and his community. He was interested, informed, and concerned about the world around him. His brow was deeply furrowed and his expression worried. He had come to me to see if acupuncture could help him, and we set up a series of appointments for treatments.

We also talked about the possible role of stress in his symptoms, and I suggested that he take home a tape of the relaxation technique you will learn later in this chapter and listen to it twice daily. The next week he came in for his first acupuncture treatment and happily reported he was "already 90 percent better." He had been enjoying his relaxation and had noticed a major improvement in his symptoms. After a few acupuncture treatments he was free of headaches and allergy symptoms. He has continued to use the relaxation tape regularly and in ten years has had no sinus infections, rare mild headaches, and needs no medications. He comes for an acupuncture treatment every year or two if the pollution levels are unusually high and his nose gets stuffy. He feels that learning to relax made a bigger change in his health than anything else he had ever experienced.

Lita, a pleasant but anxious woman, was in her thirties and had been seeing a urologist for several years for dilatation (stretching) of her urethra. The procedure was uncomfortable and she dreaded it, but it would relieve the difficulty she experienced in urinating for about six weeks each time. She had been examined by two specialists and was told that a stricture in her urethra was causing her symptoms, and she would probably always need periodic dilatation. Learning to relax appealed to Lita as a way to reduce her anxiety about the dilatation procedure. She hoped that if she was less tense, the procedure would be less painful. Neither of us thought of relaxation as a treatment for her primary problem, yet since she began a regular relaxation practice over ten years ago, she has not had further difficulties in urination and has not needed a single dilatation. She might never have needed it if she or her doctors had been educated about stress and relaxation.

These two cases are examples of the kind of relief that may occur when you begin to relax and allow the natural healing capabilities within you to work.

I have often thought that if I, as a physician, were limited to only one therapeutic intervention with which to treat all the people who came to see me, I would choose physiologic relaxation. Relaxation is an antidote to the taxing effects of unrelieved stress, a significant factor in most modern illnesses. Over three-quarters of all people who develop significant physical illness have unusually high levels of stress in the year preceding their illness.[1]

What Is Stress?

Stress and its effects are known to be causative, precipitating, and aggravating factors in illnesses as varied as heart disease, cancer, arthritis, diabetes, hyperthyroidism, gastritis, esophagitis, ulcers, colitis, hay fever, asthma, eczema, and sinusitis; as well as in common symptoms such as headaches, neck pain, back pain, dizziness, weakness, fatigue, anxiety, susceptibility to colds and viruses, menstrual irregularities, chronic vaginal and reproductive-system infections, infertility, impotence, and a host of less well-defined syndromes.[2]

Dr. Hans Selye, who coined the term "stress" in the 1930s, described stress as the "rate of wear and tear" on the body. That rate is affected by our characteristic way of responding to the natural demands for adaptation and change inherent in life. Selye identified and described a pattern of physiologic response which he termed the "General Adaptation Syndrome," more commonly known as the "fight or flight" response. This response is nature's way of preparing us to meet a challenge or threat. A serious threat, such as encountering a predator in the wild or being confronted by a mugger, stimulates a pattern of physiologic reflexes in your body designed to help you survive. Your heart rate and blood pressure increase, and your muscles tense in anticipation of a furious bout of either running or fighting. Your blood is shunted away from your skin and digestive organs into your muscles, and clotting factors are activated so you can stop bleeding quickly in case of injury. Your pupils open wide, and all your senses are sharpened. In extreme cases, your bladder or bowels empty reflexively. Adrenaline and other stress-related hormones are pumped into your bloodstream to provide extra energy. All these changes have one purpose—your survival.

In the above scenarios, the outcome will probably be decided fairly rapidly. Within twenty minutes or so, you have either run or fought for your life, and in doing so, have burned up the adrenaline and related hormones of stress. Your body would then lapse (or collapse) into a compensatory period of relaxation, a period of let-down in which it can turn its energy to repair and healing.

In day-to-day life, however, sources of stress are not usually as well-defined as tigers or muggers. The demands, real or imagined, of schedules, deadlines, mortgage payments, children, and relationships merge with the almost constant background threats of pollu-tion, crime, inflation, and nuclear annihilation to create a high ambient level of tension in our society. Many of these sources of stress can be neither fought nor fled, and require that we use different coping skills in order to be able to live with them without succumbing to illness. Unless we interrupt the tension states that arise in response to these insidious stressors, we can easily find ourselves living in a continual state of physiologic alarm, and literally stew in our own stress hormones.

Dr. Selye describes the stress syndrome occurring in three phases: the immediate state of alarm, the phase of resistance to the stress, and finally a stage of exhaus-tion. During the first two stages you become aware of and grapple with the stress. If the struggle persists too long, however, exhaustion ensues. You are no longer able to maintain a high level of resistance and systems begin to break down. In this stage, you become increas-ingly vulnerable to illness.

Stress management is an important aspect of mod-ern life and consists basically of two complementary strategies: 1) Changing what can be changed externally to reduce the sources of stress and 2) Changing your attitudes and physiologic responses to those things that can't be changed. One important means of reducing the taxing effects of stress on your system is learning and using an effective relaxation technique. Physiologic relaxation is in many ways the opposite of the "fight or flight" response to stress. It allows your body to replenish, repair, and restore itself efficiently during periods of inactivity. Regular relaxation interrupts the energy drain of chronic stress. It helps you conserve and build energy that your body can use for healing.

An Energy Model of Stress

I had the pleasure of practicing in Sausalito, California, with a physician and master acupuncturist named Hal Bailen. Dr. Bailen developed an extremely useful model for stress management based on the precepts of traditional Chinese medicine.

The "One Law" of Chinese medicine states, "There is only energy and the laws it obeys." This law, forming the basis of a medical tradition that is at least ten thousand years old, is fully congruent with our current understanding of the physical universe. Physicists since Albert Einstein describe the physical world, which includes our bodies, as a complex, interweaving organization of energy in changing states of relationship and transformation. Life, at its most basic physical level, is a process of energy exchange. Life as energy is not a metaphysical concept; it is our current state of scientific knowledge.

Nonetheless, life energy, or "Chi," as it is called in Chinese medicine, is essentially a mystery. We know neither its origins nor its purpose, except according to our personal faith. It seems qualitatively different than any other form of energy known and is particularly characterized by its ability to create increasingly complex organizations of matter and energy.

The Chinese tradition states that we are all born with an energy inheritance, which is called "ancestral energy." This ancestral, constitutional energy is finite and cannot be increased. When it is depleted, we die. This initial deposit of life energy is supplemented and surrounded by energy we build through what we eat and breathe. This second energy supply can be spent but can also be replenished.

Dr. Bailen suggests you think of your ancestral energy as your savings account and the rest as your checking account. The goal is to live as much as possible from your checking account—making regular deposits, keeping enough on balance to cover your expenditures, and spending wisely. Eating good-quality food, breathing deeply and well, and exercising can build your energy checking account. High levels of stress make inordinate demands on your resources, and energy is spent more rapidly than usual. If your expenditures exceed your income, you will start bouncing "energy checks" and will need to draw from your savings account. An illness could be seen as an overdraft notice, signaling that your account is depleted, and a deposit is required. With the rest often forced by illness your system can rebuild its reserves and resume business. If you repeatedly overdraw your account, you could be closed out by the bank.

Interestingly, Hans Selye, in his first book, *The Stress of Life,* talked about energetics in a similar way. He referred to the "energy of adaptation" and conjectured that we all had a finite amount of this energy.

Conserving it, and using it wisely, led to satisfaction and perhaps longevity, while worrying it away led to premature and perhaps unnecessary illness.

From this viewpoint, relaxation techniques can be seen as ways of conserving energy. Metabolism is significantly altered in the direction of energy conservation when you relax. Oxygen consumption and carbon dioxide elimination are reduced, both indicating a slowing of metabolism in the cells. Heart rate and blood pressure go down, brain rhythms slow, and muscle tension is reduced. The net effect is a reduction in the output of energy—energy that can be used to support your health and healing.

Preparing to Relax

The relaxation method I will teach you in this chapter begins with a variation of a method called Progressive Muscular Relaxation, originated by a physician named Edmund Jacobsen in the 1930s. Jacobsen, a pioneer in muscle physiology research at Harvard, Cornell, and the University of Chicago, found that levels of muscular tension could be altered when people imagined themselves performing various events. He placed electrodes on muscles and had people imagine walking. The EMG (which measures electrical activity in the muscles) showed electrical signals in the walking muscles alone! Similarly, if he had people imagine eating a sandwich, their jaw muscles would become unconsciously activated. Jacobsen saw muscular tension as a major problem in a wide variety of medical complaints and devised a systematic method for teaching people to relax.³ While there are many other effective relaxation techniques, simplified variations of Jacobsen's method are probably the most commonly used and easily learned forms of relaxation practice. The technique is easy to learn, easy to do, and it works.

Make sure you have a quiet, private place to relax and arrange to have at least twenty-five uninterrupted minutes. Take the phone off the hook, or turn on the answering machine. If you live with other people, tell them you don't want to be disturbed unless there is a true emergency. Wear comfortable clothing, and loosen anything that is tight or restrictive. Dim the lighting. Make your environment as conducive to relaxation as you can. Once you've mastered relaxation, you will be able to use it on the commuter train or in the midst of a busy day, but until then, make it as easy as possible for yourself.

Most people find it easiest to relax lying down, face up, while others prefer sitting in a comfortable chair or cross-legged on the floor. At first, take whichever position makes it easiest for you. You can shift or move around any time in order to become even more comfortable. Sometimes people find it so easy to relax when lying down that they fall asleep during the practice. If this happens with you, then practice sitting up. Falling asleep will not harm you, but you won't get all the benefits of deep relaxation, and you won't be able to use this quiet, focused state for imagery if you are not awake.

This script, like all the others in this book, can be used in several ways. The least effective way is to slowly read the script to yourself, either mentally or out loud, pausing to sense the suggested relaxation at the end of each phrase. This is difficult because reading tends to draw your attention away from the experience of relaxation. It's better to record the script on a cassette or tape player, reading it slowly, pausing at the end of each phrase, and using a soothing, relaxing tone of voice. If this is difficult, or if your voice is not soothing to you, perhaps you have a friend with a calming voice who will record the script for you. A third option is to use the prerecorded tapes I use with my patients.

Whichever route you choose, remember that relaxation is a learned skill, like typing, playing a musical instrument, or playing any sport that requires coordination. You improve with practice, and the more you practice, the more rapidly you'll improve. Since relaxation takes advantage of a natural response, it is easier to learn than most things you have already learned, and most people become quite confident of their relaxation abilities within two weeks of regular practice.

SCRIPT:

Basic Relaxation

Prepare to relax by taking a comfortable position . . . loosen any tight or restrictive clothing . . . and make sure you will be undisturbed for about twenty to thirty minutes . . . remember, relaxation is something that happens all by itself if you let it . . . and learning to relax is learning to allow relaxation to happen . . . no one really knows exactly how you relax, but as you think relaxing thoughts, your body responds by letting go . . . we don't really know exactly how you walk, or talk, or scratch your head . . . you just decide to do these things, and your body responds . . . in the same way, it responds to your decision to let go and relax . . . as you learn to relax, please don't concern yourself with how quickly you are relaxing, or whether or not you are relaxing deeply enough . . . you will find, as you practice relaxation, that at different times you will relax at different rates . . . sometimes relaxation will occur slowly and subtly . . . other times you will relax very deeply, very quickly . . . and it really doesn't matter how you relax or how deeply you relax at this time . . . just that you notice how relaxation feels to you when it does occur . . . as you begin to let go and begin to notice the sensations of relaxation that you have. . . .

As you practice relaxation, you will find yourself relaxing more easily, more quickly, as you become more familiar with how it feels . . . as you relax and let go of any tension you feel in your body, you may find numerous benefits such as becoming more relaxed in general . . . or becoming more easily able to cope with and deal with the stresses of everyday life . . . you may be able to relax parts of your body that have become painful through chronic tension or stress, and reach even deeper levels of relaxation. . . .

Remember, if you can shift your position to become even more comfortable, please go ahead and do so . . . it will only help you relax more easily . . . the more comfortable you get, the deeper you can relax. . . .

You might like to know that when you relax, you need not lose your awareness of your surroundings . . .

and just as a sleeping mother can ignore traffic sounds
all night long, yet awaken at the first soft murmur of
her infant child, your unconscious mind can monitor
your surroundings, allowing you to relax in safety . . .
you can allow outside sounds and noises to be there in
the background of your awareness, since they are of no
importance at all to you now . . . yet if there were ever
any threat or danger to you while you were relaxing,
you would be aware of that, and come instantly
awake, alert, and capable of dealing with the
situation. . . .

Knowing this, you can begin to relax more deeply
by taking a couple of deep, slow breaths, and as you let
go and exhale, let it be a real "letting go" kind of
breath . . . and imagine yourself beginning to release
any tension or stress you may feel in your body . . .
you may want to imagine that as you breathe in, you
fill yourself with clean, fresh air and energy . . . and as
you breathe out, you release tension and discomfort
. . . just imagine it in some way leaving your body
with your breath . . . no need to force it . . . just
imagine it . . . breathing in energy and breathing out
tension . . . good . . . (allow time for three to six such
breath cycles) . . . now let your breathing return to its
natural rate and rhythm . . . breathing is a good example of an automatic process . . . so many millions and
billions of automatic processes happening in your body
every moment of every day . . . your heart beating
. . . your blood circulating to every part of your body
. . . the wondrously complex chemical reactions happening in every cell . . . all happening without you
ever having to know exactly how it happens . . . and in

the same way, relaxation happens . . . and feeling more comfortable . . .

And now focus your awareness on your left foot . . . merely notice any tension that may be there . . . and invite your left foot to relax . . . and let go of that tension . . . letting go of any tension you may be holding in your left foot . . . releasing and relaxing . . . allowing your left foot to relax more comfortably . . . without any concern for how deeply or comfortably your left foot goes . . . just noticing the sensations of letting go in that foot . . . the feelings of letting go . . . now . . . in your left foot . . . allowing your foot to reach a deeper and more comfortable state of ease . . . a really enjoyable and pleasant feeling of relaxation beginning to deepen in that foot. . . .

And now, notice any tension you may be holding in your right foot . . . and release and relax your right foot . . . and notice any sensations of relaxation beginning to deepen in your right foot . . . in both your feet . . . as you allow your feet to head for a deeper and more comfortable state of relaxation . . . knowing that at any time, when you relax any part of you, the rest of you relaxes more deeply as well . . . and as you allow the relaxation in your feet to deepen, notice any tension you may be holding in your left calf . . . releasing and relaxing any tension you may be holding in the muscles of your left calf . . . just letting go . . . and allowing it to relax . . . not really worrying about how it relaxes . . . and notice any tension you may be holding in your right calf muscles . . . and allow that to release and relax . . . release and relax the muscles of your right calf . . . noticing the sensations of relaxing

in your calf muscles . . . spreading down through your
ankles and your feet . . . and allowing that sensation of
relaxation in your lower legs to deepen and continue as
you notice any tension you may be holding in the
muscles of your left thigh . . . the large muscles of
your left thigh . . . that do so much work during the
day . . . and release and relax the muscles of your left
thigh . . . as you let go more easily and deeply . . .
notice any tension you may be holding in your right
thigh muscles . . . release and relax the muscles of your
right thigh . . . allowing your thighs to release more
deeply and comfortably and noticing the sensations of
comfort and release as they occur . . . deepening sensations of relaxation . . . just letting go, letting it deepen
. . . almost as if it was happening all by itself. . . .

When you give it permission to relax, your body
relaxes . . . notice the pleasure and comfort, the enjoyable feeling of letting go . . . and relaxing more deeply
. . . and allowing that sensation of relaxation in your
legs to deepen. . . .

Bring your attention to the muscles of your low
back and buttocks . . . notice any tension in this very
important part of your body . . . this hard-working
part of your body . . . and release and relax any tension
you may be holding in this area of your body . . .
allowing those muscles to take a well-deserved rest . . .
just letting go of any unnecessary tension and stress in
that part of your body . . . and noticing the pleasant
sensations of relaxation coming into the large muscles
of your lower back and buttocks . . . notice any tension you may be holding in your pelvis and around
your genitals . . . allow that area of your body to

release and relax . . . feeling a deeper and more comfortable sense of relaxation coming through your
pelvis, your genital area . . . the whole lower part of
your body . . . now . . . going deeper and better relaxed . . . to a more comfortable level of body and
mind . . . release and relax any tension you may be
holding in the muscles of your midback and abdomen
. . . allowing this area of your body to join in the sense
of deeper, more comfortable relaxation . . . release and
relax any tension you may be holding in the organs in
your abdominal cavity . . . feeling the entire abdomen
relaxing more deeply . . . easily . . . comfortably . . .
release and relax any tension you may be holding in the
muscles of your chest . . . and in the organs in your
chest . . . in the muscles between and over your shoulder blades . . . allow your entire chest to relax easily
. . . deeply . . . comfortably . . . allowing the relaxation to deepen in every part of you as well . . . not too
deeply . . . just deeply enough for you to feel most
comfortable . . . in your shoulders . . . the muscles of
your shoulders relaxing and letting go . . . releasing
and relaxing any tension in the muscles of your shoulders . . . and your upper arms . . . allowing your upper
arms to join in this pleasant and enjoyable sense of
letting go . . . letting go of any tension in your arms
and your elbows . . . releasing and relaxing any tension
you may feel in your forearms . . . wrists . . . and
down into your hands . . . notice any tension in your
hands, in the many small muscles in your hands . . .
and inviting your hands to let go . . . to join in this
deeper and more comfortable state of relaxation . . .
notice the pleasant feelings of relaxation in each indi-

vidual finger . . . your index fingers relaxing . . . your
middle fingers relaxing . . . your ring fingers . . . your
little fingers . . . your thumbs deeply and comfortably
at ease. . . .

Now notice any tension you may be holding in
the muscles of your neck . . . the muscles that hold
your head up all day . . . and allow them now to take a
well-deserved rest . . . releasing any tension you may
be holding in your neck . . . just allowing it to go
easily and naturally . . . inviting your neck to join with
the deep, comfortable state of relaxation you feel in
other parts of your body. . . .

And now release and relax any tension you may
feel in your scalp and forehead . . . notice a comfortable sense of relaxation beginning to come into the
muscles of your scalp and forehead, flowing down
through the muscles of your face . . . your cheeks . . .
your jaw . . . relaxing your jaws . . . feeling a releasing
and ease in your face . . . releasing any tension you
may feel in the little muscles around your eyes . . .
allowing them to let go and imagine that pleasant sense
of softening flowing down through your face . . . your
neck . . . your shoulders . . . and all the way through
your body . . . a very pleasant, comfortable, and deep
sense of relaxation. . . .

And you may be finding that as your body has
become more relaxed . . . your mind, too, has become
more quiet . . . and still . . . and please take a few
moments and enjoy this deeper, more comfortable
state of body and mind . . . allowing your mind to
become quiet . . . and calm . . . and still . . . allowing
the relaxation to deepen. . . .

Good . . . you will find that each time you practice relaxation you will be able to relax more quickly . . . more easily . . . and more deeply. . . .

Relaxation is something you learn . . . like playing a piano . . . or driving a car . . . or playing a game . . . and you get better and better as you do it more and more. . . .

Now to bring yourself awake . . . but bringing back with you a comfortable sense of this relaxation . . . all you need to do is count upward mentally from one to five . . . picture each number in your mind as you count up . . . and when you reach the number five, you can find yourself wide-awake, alert, relaxed, and feeling better than before . . . you may feel refreshed as if you had just had a deep, refreshing sleep . . . you will come wide-awake and alert, ready to go about your day, when you reach the number five . . . in a moment, I will count from one to five, and you can come back wide-awake, feeling refreshed, relaxed, and better than before . . . picture the number one in your mind's eye and begin to come back to your awareness of the outside world . . . see the number two and come more awake, sensing your body light and free of tension . . . see the number three and become aware of the room you are in, the sounds around you, and imagine you are waking up from a deeply refreshing nap . . . when you reach five, you can come fully awake and aware . . . see the number four and come more awake and alert . . . see the number five, and your eyes can open, and you may want to stretch and smile to come all the way back . . . refreshed, relaxed, and feeling better than before. . . .

Evaluating Your Experience

When you come fully awake, take a few minutes to write about your experience. Which parts of your body relaxed most easily? Which took longer, or didn't feel completely relaxed?

What was most interesting to you about the process? How relaxed were you? Did anything interfere with your ability to relax, and if so, how will you deal with that next time you practice?

Notice how you feel right after relaxation and an hour or so later. Compare how you feel after relaxing to how you felt before you started. Are you more comfortable? Did you have any pain or tension when you started that isn't there now? Do you feel more refreshed?

If you feel logy or tired after relaxation, take more time to fully bring yourself out of the relaxation state. It will help to count upwards again from one to five, and to stretch, clench your fists, or clap your hands to bring yourself all the way wide awake.

How Often Should I Practice?

If you have a health-related problem, you should practice relaxation at least twice a day, taking about twenty to twenty-five minutes per session. Morning and late-afternoon sessions seem to work best for most people. The morning session puts you in a relaxed, yet alert frame of mind, which often helps the day run smoothly. The afternoon session lets you release accumulated tension from the day and makes the evenings more pleasant. Some people find that relaxation helps them fall asleep if they practice at bedtime, but others find that it energizes them and keeps them awake. Experiment on your own to find the best times for you to practice.

If you relax regularly for two to three weeks you'll condition your system to relax on cue and will find yourself more relaxed in general. Practice the Basic Relaxation exercise until you feel confident that your body relaxes when you give it the chance. Then go on to the Deepening exercises described in the next chapter.

NOTES

1) Rahe, R. H., Meyer, M., Smith, M., Kjaer, G., and Holmes, T. H. 1964, "Social stress and illness onset." *Journal of Psychosomatic Research,* 8:35–44.

2) Literally hundreds of books and articles cover the adverse effects of excessive stress on health. Two of the best are *Mind as Healer, Mind as Slayer,* Delta, 1977, and *Holistic Medicine,* Delacorte/Lawrence, 1979, both by Kenneth Pelletier. Both are well-documented yet eminently readable.

3) Jacobsen, Edmund, M.D., (1962). *You Must Relax.* New York: McGraw-Hill Book Company.

FIVE

Going Deeper Within

While relaxation is often the beginning of healing, it won't cure everything, and it won't solve all your problems. There are, however, benefits of relaxation that extend beyond its ability to relieve tension patterns. These effects make it even more valuable as a foundation upon which to build your self-healing abilities.

1) Learning to relax builds confidence in your ability to control your body, your feelings, and your thoughts. You become aware of having *more choice* in how you react and how you feel.

2) Relaxing helps you become *more aware* of what kinds of things, people, and thoughts tend to make you tense. This is the first step in being able to deal with them constructively.

3) Relaxation interrupts habitual negative thought patterns and autosuggestions. It *clears your mind* and *opens it to new ideas,* new possibilities, and new ways of solving old problems. It allows you to draw on your intuition and creativity to help you move in the direction you want to go.

4) Deep relaxation *provides a state of mind in which*

more advanced and specific imagery techniques are most effective.

Let's look more closely at how each of these benefits can help you in your movement toward healing:

1) *Having a Choice in How You Feel*

Learning to relax at will gives you a sense of confidence in your ability to focus your mind and influence your body. The sense of being out of control is frequently one of the most distressing aspects of being ill. When you learn to change your physiologic state from distress to peacefulness you are no longer powerless.

Barry, an insurance agent with neck tension and pain, knew that his job was his major source of stress. He experienced a lot of pain relief from practicing relaxation. After a few weeks of practice he also said, "I used to think it was my boss who got me uptight. Now I see it's my reaction to him, and I don't *have to* get uptight when he walks through the office or says something to me. He can still get to me if he criticizes me, but now I can let go of it pretty quickly by practicing my relaxation method. I feel a lot freer than I did before, and less trapped by my tension."

Knowing how to relax can be a blessing even in the worst situations. Three years ago I was called to see a woman who was in the Intensive Care Unit. Her husband, her internist, and her lung specialist had all asked me to see if there was anything I could do for her. Martha was in her thirties, the mother of two small children, and was suffering from a uniformly fatal lung

disease. Her lungs were becoming progressively thick-
ened and her breathing increasingly inefficient and difficult. She had lost 30 of her usual 120 pounds and had
been hospitalized for weeks in the ICU. She had tubes in
her nose, mouth, bladder, and both arms, through
which she was fed, oxygenated, hydrated, and relieved
of urine. Her doctor said she had been vomiting every
two hours for several days and was asking for higher
levels of pain medications, which further inhibited her
breathing. She became disoriented several times and
tore out her IV tubes and oxygen, so the nurses had to
restrain her by tying her to the bed. The doctors and
nurses in the ICU who deal with death and tragedy on a
daily basis were almost overcome with a sense of help-
lessness and grief.

I went to see her with a sense of dread. I felt like I
was being called on to perform a miracle and was
acutely aware of my lack of that ability. I spent about
two hours with her, just talking and listening. We
established a good rapport and talked about her college
days in Berkeley, about her marriage, her children, her
parents, and her feelings about her situation. Finally I
said, "I can't promise you magic, but would you like to
learn to become more comfortable?" She readily
agreed, and I led her through the Basic Relaxation
exercise you have learned. She easily drifted into the
most serene state of relaxation you can possibly imagine
and soon fell asleep.

I told the nursing staff and house staff what had
happened, and left a relaxation tape there for her to play
whenever she felt like it. Four days later she died, as
expected. The nurses reported she had not vomited

again after learning to "become more comfortable" and hadn't become disoriented and agitated. She had asked for no pain medication in the four days. She had spent most of the time with her eyes closed, looking peaceful and content, and had been able to talk at length with her husband and children before she died. Martha showed me that even in the worst of circumstances there may be choice and comfort, through very simple means.

2) Identifying Sources of Tension

When you learn what relaxation feels like, you are better able to sense the contrasting feelings of tension. This allows you to more accurately identify what makes you tense. This can be the beginning of being able to deal with stress more effectively.

Judith, a suburban mother, never noticed how tense she was while driving until she began practicing relaxation techniques. Soon afterward she began to notice that her shoulders became tense and painful within ten minutes of beginning to drive. Once she noticed that, she found it was easy to shrug her shoulders and let them relax. After two weeks of relaxation practice and letting go of her habitual tension, she found herself naturally more relaxed and comfortable while driving.

3) Enhanced Creativity and Problem-Solving Ability

Creativity and healing are closely related. Both involve bringing things together in new ways. New tissue is created as part of the physical repair process.

New perspectives, which often emerge spontaneously during relaxation, may lead to changes in thinking and lifestyle patterns that can promote healing.

Biofeedback research at the Menninger Foundation in Kansas has shown that people who train themselves to maintain a certain brain-wave rhythm (theta rhythm, six to eight cycles per second) often experience spontaneous insight into matters of importance to them.[1] Deep relaxation slows your brain-wave pattern to rhythms bordering on theta and may result in the spontaneous realization of something important to you for healing. Don't struggle or try to have new thoughts as you relax, but be aware that they may occur. Later, you will learn imagery techniques specifically aimed at stimulating this kind of insight.

4) Relaxation Sets the Stage for Skillful Imaging

Relaxation techniques are the first step in learning to use your images, thoughts, and feelings skillfully. The ability to quiet your mind and concentrate your attention will enable you to make the best use of the more advanced techniques you will learn in the following chapters.

Deepening Your Relaxation With Imagery

Once you've developed some confidence in your ability to relax it's time to learn to deepen your relaxation. The simple deepening methods I will teach you build on the basic skills you have already learned. They will help you to deepen your inner concentration, which will improve your responsiveness to the images you will create in later exercises.

The Deepening Technique script will again guide you through your body, inviting each part to relax, and then add two simple imagery techniques for deepening. First, you will imagine yourself walking down a staircase, with each step taking you a little deeper and better relaxed, and then you will imagine yourself in a beautiful, peaceful, serene, and safe inner place. In this exercise, there is less introductory material, and you can move through your body a little more rapidly than before. This exercise now replaces your Basic Relaxation exercise.

As with all the scripts in this book, you may want to read it slowly to yourself, and go along with the suggestions, have a friend read it to you, make a tape you can listen to, or use the prerecorded tapes that are available. Take a comfortable position and make sure you will have about twenty-five minutes of uninterrupted time.

SCRIPT:

Deepening Techniques

Begin to relax by taking a comfortable position . . . loosening any tight or restrictive clothing or jewelry . . . and making sure you won't be disturbed for about twenty minutes . . . take a couple of deep, slow breaths and let the out breaths be real "letting go" kinds of breaths . . . as if you are beginning to release any tension or discomfort in your body. . . .

Now that you have learned to relax, you will find your body and mind relax more quickly and more easily than ever before . . . as you focus your attention on each part of your body, you can invite it to release and relax any tension that may be there, and then merely allow it to release in its own way. . . .

Focus your awareness on your left foot, and invite your left foot to release and relax any tension it may be holding . . . notice the beginning sensations of relaxation in that foot . . . in the same way, invite your right foot to release and relax any tension that might be there . . . invite the muscles of your left calf and shin to release . . . and your right calf and shin . . . just notice and allow your lower legs to relax in their own way, becoming more comfortable and at ease all the while. . . .

Remember, as each part of you relaxes, all of you relaxes more deeply, and as you relax more deeply, each part can relax even more easily. . . .

Invite your left thigh and hamstrings to release and relax . . . and your right thigh and hamstrings . . . allow your hips and pelvis to join in this letting go and releasing of tension . . . allow your entire lower body to release and relax . . . and notice the relaxing sensations . . . allow it to be a comfortable and pleasant experience . . . invite your low back and buttocks to join in releasing and relaxing any tension that may be there . . . and your genital area. . . .

Invite your abdomen to relax . . . the muscles of your abdomen and your midback . . . to join in this

deeper, more comfortable state of relaxation . . . invite
the organs in your abdominal cavity to also join in this
letting go, this release . . . and just allow that whole
lower half of your body to let go and become even
more deeply comfortable and at ease . . . invite your
chest muscles and the muscles between your shoulder
blades to release and relax . . . becoming soft and at
ease . . . the organs in your chest joining in this deeper,
more comfortable state. . . .

Imagine your shoulders and neck muscles becoming soft, releasing any tension that may be there . . .
allowing them to take a well-deserved rest . . . and this
relaxation flowing down over your shoulders into your
upper arms . . . elbows . . . forearms . . . wrists . . .
and hands. . . .

Invite all the small muscles of your hands . . . in
between the fingers . . . to release and relax and become very comfortable and deeply relaxed . . . your
index fingers . . . middle fingers . . . ring fingers . . .
little fingers . . . and your thumbs . . . deeply relaxed
. . . all the way to the very tips. . . .

Allow your scalp and forehead to release and relax
any tension that may be there . . . becoming soft and
smooth and at ease . . . the muscles of your face soft
and at ease . . . and allowing a very pleasant sense of
relaxation to come into the small muscles all around
your eyes . . . inviting those muscles to release any
tension and to feel that sense of letting go flowing
through your face and jaws . . . neck and shoulders
. . . and all the way down. . . .

And as your body relaxes more deeply, your mind
becomes quiet and peaceful as well. . . .

Now to deepen this comfortable state of relaxa-

tion and concentration, imagine yourself at the top of a
stairway that has ten steps leading down from where
you stand . . . let it be any kind of stairway . . . one
you've seen before or one you just make up . . . and
take some time to observe it in detail . . . notice what
the stairs are made of . . . how steep or shallow they
are . . . how wide or how narrow . . . do they go
straight down, do they spiral, or is there a landing
halfway down? . . . Are the stairs covered with anything? . . . What is the texture beneath your feet? . . . Is
there a bannister or handrail to hold as you go down?

When you are ready, begin to descend the staircase
one step at a time, counting backward from ten to one
as you go, one number per step . . . allowing yourself
to feel more deeply, more comfortably relaxed with
each step you descend . . . let this imaginary staircase
help you reach an even deeper, more comfortable level
of body and mind with each step down . . . ten . . .
nine . . . deeper and more comfortably relaxed . . .
eight . . . each step takes you deeper . . . seven . . . and
six . . . easily and naturally . . . five . . . halfway down
. . . with nothing to worry . . . nothing to bother . . .
four . . . deeper . . . more comfortably relaxed . . .
three . . . no need to worry about exactly how deeply
or how comfortably you go . . . two . . . and one . . .
at the bottom of the stairs . . . very comfortable and
deeply relaxed in body and mind. . . .

To further deepen your relaxation, imagine yourself now in a very beautiful, peaceful place. . . . This
might be somewhere you've visited before or somewhere you just make up in your imagination . . . just
let the image of the place come to you. . . . It really
doesn't matter what kind of place you imagine as long

as it's beautiful, quiet, peaceful, and serene. . . . Let
this be a special inner place for you . . . somewhere
that you feel particularly at ease . . . a place where you
feel secure and at one with your surroundings . . .
maybe you've had a place like this in your life . . .
somewhere you go to to be quiet and reflective . . .
somewhere special and healing for you . . . or it could
be a place you've seen in a movie . . . or read about
. . . or just dreamed of . . . it could be a real place, like
a meadow, or a beach . . . or an imaginary place like
floating on a soft cloud. . . .

Let yourself explore whatever quiet imaginary
place you go to as if you were there now . . . notice
what you see there . . . what sounds you hear . . . even
the smells or aromas that you sense there . . . notice
especially what it feels like to be there, and immerse
yourself in the beauty, the feelings of peacefulness . . .
of being secure and at ease. . . .

As you explore this special inner place, find a spot
that feels particularly good to be in . . . a spot where
you feel especially calm . . . centered . . . and at ease
. . . let yourself become comfortable and centered in
this spot . . . let this be your "power spot"—a place in
which you draw from the deep sense of peacefulness
you feel here . . . a place of healing . . . and of rest . . .
and a place where you can explore and use the power
of your imagination to best effect. . . .

Take some time to relax into the deep feelings of
peacefulness, quiet, and healing you can sense in this
spot . . . take as much time as you need. . . .

When you are ready, prepare yourself to come
back to your waking state . . . remember, this is your
special inner place, a place you can return to at any

time of your own choosing . . . a place within where
rest, healing, and peace are always available . . . a place
that is always with you . . . and a place you can draw
from when these qualities are needed. . . .

To return to waking, but bringing back with you
the sense of peacefulness and healing you have experienced here . . . all you need to do is to recall the imaginary staircase you descended . . .imagine yourself at
the bottom of the stairs . . . with ten steps up . . . as
you ascend the stairs, you become more and more
wide-awake, alert, and aware of your surroundings
. . . when you reach ten, the top of the stairs, let yourself come wide-awake, alert, and refreshed . . . feeling
better than before. . . .

. . . one . . . two . . . coming up, coming more
awake . . . three . . . four . . . bringing back with you a
sense of peace, of relaxation . . . five . . . when you
reach ten you may open your eyes, stretch, and come
all the way wide-awake . . . six . . . feeling refreshed as
if you had a very good nap . . . seven . . . at ten you
will be wide-awake and alert, feeling very good and
refreshed . . . eight . . . your eyes may start to feel like
they want to open . . . nine . . . and ten . . . at the top
of the stairs and wide-awake. . . .

Open your eyes . . . stretch . . . smile . . . and
come alert, refreshed, and wide-awake again.

Evaluating Your Experience

Again, take a few minutes to write about your
experience. Were you able to imagine descending the
staircase? What was it like? Could you feel or imagine

yourself going deeper as you moved down the stairs? Did the experience seem to change in any way as you moved down?

What was your quiet inner place like? Was it new or familiar to you? Do you have any particular associations or memories connected to this place? How did it feel to imagine yourself there?

If you didn't feel you found a suitable quiet place, read on for some suggestions that will help you do that.

Several pointers may help you use this Deepening Technique more effectively. First, remember that this is a skill you are developing. Take your time with it, and experiment until it works well for you. Some people, for instance, find that going down twenty stairs helps them reach the most comfortable level of relaxation, while others find that just five stairs is enough. You may find you can control your depth of relaxation by varying the number of stairs you go down.

Charles, a patient with a recurrent back problem, became quite good at relieving his back muscle spasms with relaxation techniques. Once he severely sprained his back while traveling and found himself with intense pain and muscle spasms and no easy access to medical care. He tried to relax but with little success due to the severity of his pain. After several attempts, he decided to imagine a staircase with one hundred stairs, vowing to go as far down as he needed to go in order to relax. He remembers reaching the high seventies, falling asleep, and waking up a few hours later feeling considerably better.

Second, it may take some "inner traveling" before you settle on a place that feels just right. You might imagine going to several places before you find the one that feels best. It's also perfectly all right to have more than one special inner place. Remember this is your imagination—travel is cheap here, and at these prices you can afford to have a house in France and a beautiful tropical island all your own! You may find that you use different inner places for different purposes—like going to a sunny beach for rest and relaxation, but to a mountaintop to get an "overview" of a situation. Or you might be more comfortable using one special place consistently. The most important thing is to respect what feels best *to you*—this is *your* special inner place, a place of comfort, peace, and sanctuary for you. While people commonly imagine mountain lakes, tranquil meadows, quiet forest clearings and other beautiful natural settings, one patient of mine found her special place was playing slot machines in a Las Vegas casino!

It also helps you relax more deeply to imagine not only the sights you see but the sounds you hear, the aromas you smell, and the feelings you experience in your imaginary special place. Using all your senses in imagery involves more of your brain in the process and makes the imaginary experience more "real" to your lower brain centers. Thus, they are more likely to respond to those images, giving the "all-clear" message to the body, and allowing it to relax.

Once you are comfortable with your ability to relax and go to your quiet inner place, you will want to begin to experiment with creating images specifically aimed at relieving your symptoms or stimulating your healing process. The next several chapters will teach you how to do this, beginning with simple directive images and visualizations and moving to receptive imagery techniques that can help you develop a more specific vision of how to support your own healing.

NOTES

1) Green, A. M. (1974), "Brainwave training, imagery, creativity, and integrative experiences." *Proceedings of the Biofeedback Research Society*, Biofeedback Research Society, Denver.

SIX

Your Own Healing Imagery

Now that you've learned to relax, you are ready to begin using imagery in more specific ways to improve your health. Imagery is a two-way medium of communication between your silent, unconscious mind and your verbal, conscious mind. It can be used both to illuminate patterns that affect your health and to focus energy that can change those patterns.

These receptive and active modes of imaging have complementary functions in self-healing. Receptive imagery helps you become aware of unconscious patterns, needs, and potentials for change. It simply involves paying attention to the imagery that arises in response to the questions you ask in a relaxed, respectful state of mind. Active imagery, on the other hand, communicates your conscious intentions (or requests) to your unconscious mind. It, too, is a simple process which consists of imagining your desired goal as if it is already achieved while maintaining a passive, relaxed state of mind. Together, receptive and active imagery can help you create healing imagery most appropriate and effective for you.

What Are the Best Images for Healing?

Research psychologists Jeanne Achterberg and Frank Lawlis at the University of Texas Health Sciences Center at Dallas studied the imagery of cancer patients working with the Simonton method of visualization and have been able to correlate certain characteristics of their imagery with improved survival. Their findings indicate that the more powerful and active the imagery of immune system function, the better the outcome for the patient. Anatomical accuracy does not seem to be a factor in effectiveness, and, in fact, symbolic representation of the activity often seems to be more effective.[1]

Other studies, however, have shown that in some situations, imagining the anatomic and physiologic details of the healing seems to improve results. In a study conducted at the Behavioral Medicine Unit at the University of California at San Francisco, patients with asthma were taught relaxation and visualization techniques aimed at relieving their breathing difficulties. One group of patients was taught to imagine breathing easily through wide-open bronchial tubes. Another group was taught a much more detailed model of asthma. In asthmatics, certain cells (mast cells) lining the airways are hyperreactive to various stimuli. When they react, they release a chemical called histamine that causes airway constriction and difficulty in breathing. This second group of patients imagined their mast cells being calm and stable, holding their histamine inside. While both imagery groups experienced improvement in their asthma, the group visualizing stable mast cells improved more.(2)

These seemingly conflicting findings are not really contradictory. In the second study, patients didn't have the option of creating their own personalized imagery. Instead, they were taught one of two preselected imagery scenarios. I wonder how a group would have fared that was encouraged to develop a personal image of asthma and a personal image of easy breathing. Studies will soon be done to explore this issue.

My guess is that the second group in the asthma study became more deeply interested and involved with their imagery as they learned more about the nature of their illness at a cellular level. My experience is that imagery is most effective when it has personal meaning to an individual, and when it evokes a positive emotional response. The strongest images of healing feel "right" and powerful, and will cause a perceptible shift in feelings. There may even be an immediate response in sensations associated with the symptoms involved.

Not everyone will receive an image this powerful, however, at least not right away. In the absence of such an image, an anatomical image can often be effective and is an excellent place to start. When you create an image of anatomical or physiologic healing, detailed information can help make the image more powerful. Ask your doctor or health-care practitioner to explain your symptoms or illness in terms you can understand and visualize. Ask them how healing could happen if it were to occur. Look at the many anatomy and physiology guides now available—some of the best are listed in the Resource Guide. I am not sure whether it is imagining the process in detail or the willingness to invest the time and attention to learn about the detail that makes the difference, but in either case, it does seem to make a difference.

Whatever imagery you choose to focus on, frequency of practice seems to be a particularly important factor in effectiveness. People who practice their imagery most frequently and enthusiastically receive the most benefit. So when you begin to use imagery, use it often, and use it wholeheartedly.

The method you will learn in this chapter to develop your personal healing imagery is simple and direct, and makes use of both receptive and active imagery. A script follows that will lead you through the process. You will relax and go to your quiet inner place. When you are calm and centered, you will focus your attention directly on the symptoms that are most bothersome to you. If there are no symptoms associated with your illness, you can focus on the area of your body that is involved, or on the name of the illness. Once you are calmly focused, you will let an image come to mind that represents this problem or symptom. Accept whatever image comes to mind, and welcome it into your awareness. It may be familiar or strange, and you may or may not understand how it is connected to your symptom. You will let it be whatever it is and allow it to become clearer. You will observe it carefully and in detail. Then you will be asked to notice what seems to be "wrong" with this picture. What is it that seems to represent the pain, or illness, or problem? Up to this point, you have used the receptive mode of imagery.

Next you will be asked to allow another image to form that represents the healing or resolution of your problem. You will imagine the healing process taking place in whatever way seems right to you as the image of illness changes to the image of health. In the Healing Imagery script, you will be encouraged to imagine feeling positive changes happening in your body as you focus on the healing image. Notice any change in sensations and take them as signs of encouragement, of connection to the body itself.

By using receptive imagery to help you form your active imagery, you invite your silent mind to guide you in this process. You allow it to reveal its perception of the problem and the potential solution. Healing, after all, is an unconscious process, and your unconscious mind is the mind that understands it. By eliciting and affirming its own image of healing you use its native language to encourage it to carry out the process. The image you create may be anatomically accurate or purely symbolic. The most important thing is that it is *yours*.

While yours is the most important image, a few examples of images that others have created might help you realize how different and personal the imagery can be and still be effective. Consider three people with back problems.

An orthopedic surgeon friend of mind had a severely herniated lumbar disk. He was a very progressive surgeon who had used hypnosis to help his patients recover quickly from surgery, and he believed in the power of the mind to assist healing. He doubted, however, that imagery could help repair a ruptured intervertebral disk, but wanted to do anything he could to avoid surgery. He was able to visualize the disk quite well, since he had seen so many of them in his work. He described it as a fibrous sac, whose contents had "blown out" and were now pressing on a nerve in his back. He couldn't imagine a satisfactory way for it to be repaired without surgery, and became increasingly frustrated. Finally, he decided to relax very deeply and see if the image could change by itself. Suddenly he saw a vivid image of the center of the disk being sucked back into the sac, and the tear sealing itself up like the diaphragm of a camera. The image was so clear it startled him. He was even more startled to find that after this session he was greatly relieved of pain and was able to walk without pain down his leg for the first time in several weeks. He went on to recover completely without surgery, a fact that has both pleased and amazed him since.

Another friend and patient with a recurring back problem would imagine a huge rope knot representing the muscle spasms in his back. As he relaxed, he could visualize the knot loosening and found that his back muscles completely relaxed by the time he was able to imagine the knot untied.

A third patient with a one-year history of severe unremitting back pain imagined a knife stabbing him in the back. In guided imagery, he was asked to look at who put the knife there, and he saw his ex-business partner who had stolen from and ruined their business. A brief course of counseling sessions helped him express and come to terms with the feelings of anger and loss that he had been holding inside, and his back pain disappeared as he worked through his feelings.

The point here is that a similar problem may produce different images in different people, and may lead in different directions for healing. Sometimes, ac-

tive imagery will suffice to relieve pain and stimulate
healing, while in other cases receptive imagery will
point to physical, emotional, or situational problems
that need resolution before healing can proceed.

Let's look at some other images that patients of
mine have created of their illnesses and their healing
processes. Remember, while "create" is not quite the
right word—"receive" might be better—these images
came from concentrating on the problem and being
receptive to the images that formed.

A man with a painfully inflamed wrist imagined his
wrist bones having sharp, jagged edges that grated on
each other as he used his hand. In contrast, the image of
his normal wrist included rounded bones, with rubber
and cotton cushions between them, allowing smooth,
painless movement. In his Healing Imagery he imagined gently placing cushions and supports between the
bones of the painful wrist and was able to greatly reduce
his discomfort as his wrist healed. His imagery was not
anatomically correct, yet it was effective in reducing his
pain.

A young man with ulcerative colitis had been
having painful abdominal cramping and bleeding from
his rectum for two months. Medication was not helping, and he wanted to avoid cortisone if he could. He
imagined his colon being red, raw, and irritable. He said
it seemed "uptight" and "oversensitive." As he relaxed
with his hands on his abdomen, he imagined his hands
melting into his body and lovingly stroking and mas-
saging his colon. He imagined his colon relaxing and
resting in his hands. At the same time, he felt a pleasant
sense of warmth in his belly, and imagined fresh,

healthy blood flowing to his colon, refreshing, cleansing, and healing it. In two days he was free of symptoms. Three weeks later, his gastroenterologist said his colon appeared to be completly healed.

A sixty-five-year-old retired heavy equipment operator with a herniated disk in his back imagined a tiny work crew inserting house-lifting jacks between his vertebrae. He then imagined them clearing out the old "busted" disk and installing a fresh one, which he visualized as a small, very tough rubber ball. When the "work crew" lowered the top vertebra, the ball flattened into a cylindrical shock absorber, which maintained the space between the bones. He even imagined it cushioning the joint as he walked. He found this image to be a consistently effective way to relieve his back pain and sciatica.

A thirty-year-old woman with endometriosis visualized her disease as tar stuck to her pelvic organs. She imagined having a potent cleaning solution, a scraper, and a mop, and in her mind's eye cleaned up every last bit of the tar. She consistently visualized this process for fifteen minutes two or three times a day and three months later had no visible endometriosis when her gynecologist examined her through a laparoscope.

A fifty-two-year-old businessman with a peptic ulcer visualized spraying the inside of his stomach and intestines with a cooling white foam three times a day between meals and was able not only to relieve his pain but to heal quickly, discontinue his ulcer medications, and remain free of ulcers through several stressful years.

A mother of three with a week-long sinus headache focused on her pain and saw a large eye with wings on either side. As she watched it, it suddenly flew away, and a large glob of mucus fell into the back of her throat. She was surprised to sit up and find that her headache was relieved. Neither she nor I ever understood the significance of the symbol. It seemed as if the imagery itself produced relief.

A twenty-seven-year-old junior executive was having anxiety attacks at work. As he relaxed and asked for an image for his anxiety, he saw a frenetic honeybee, flying about in an agitated state. The bee seemed scattered and didn't seem to have any pattern or direction in its movement. The image for healing that came to him was a rose. He imagined holding the rose out to the bee, and it came over and began collecting nectar. The bee then seemed more relaxed and content, and so did the young man. He found this simple visualization calming and centering and used it for a few minutes at a time whenever he began to feel anxious and scattered like his imaginary bee.

In later chapters I will describe other cases where imagery has led people to a deeper understanding of how they could contribute to their own healing. The script that follows, however, will allow you to begin using both receptive and active imagery to begin that process. As with all the imagery exercises in this book, let this be an exploration, and remember there is no right or wrong imagery to have. Be respectful of your own imagery, and carefully observe what comes.

You may use the script that follows as you have the others, making sure you have a comfortable quiet space in which to concentrate, and about twenty minutes of uninterrupted time.

SCRIPT:

Healing Imagery

Begin by taking a couple of deep, full breaths . . . and let the out breath be a real "letting go" kind of breath . . . make sure you are comfortable . . . and that you won't be disturbed for twenty minutes or so. . . .

As you breathe comfortably and easily, invite your body to relax and let go of any unnecessary tension . . . take the time to bring your attention to each part of your body, and invite it to release and relax as you have so many times before. . . .

Release and relax any tension you may have in your left foot . . . your right foot . . . your calves . . . your thighs and hamstrings . . . your hips . . . pelvis . . . genitals . . . low back . . . buttocks. . . .

Take your time and sense the comfortable feelings of deepening relaxation beginning in the lower half of your body . . . easily . . . naturally . . . invite your abdomen to release and relax and join in this more comfortable and pleasant state of relaxation . . . the organs within your abdomen . . . your midback and flanks . . . your chest . . . the muscles across and between your shoulder blades . . . deeper and more comfortably at ease . . . the organs in your chest . . . breathing easily and naturally . . . your shoulders . . . and neck . . . relaxing more deeply, more comfortably, more easily. . . .

As each part relaxes, you relax more deeply . . . and as you go deeper, it is easier to relax. . . . The

relaxation is flowing down your upper arms . . . your
elbows . . . forearms . . . wrists . . . and hands . . .
sense the relaxation in the small muscles between your
fingers . . . and all the way to the tips of the index
fingers . . . the middle fingers . . . ring fingers . . . little
fingers . . . and thumbs . . .

Scalp and forehead soft and relaxed . . . the muscles of the face soft and at ease . . . the little muscles
around the eyes relaxing more deeply . . . more pleasantly . . . more comfortably. . . .

And imagine yourself at the top of your imaginary
staircase that leads to an even deeper and more comfortable state of mind and body . . . notice what it
looks like today . . . and descend one step at a time . . .
going deeper, more comfortably relaxed with each
descending stair . . . let it be an enjoyable experience
. . . head for that special inner place of peacefulness and
healing you have visited before. . . .

Ten . . . nine . . . deeper, more comfortably
relaxed as you go down the stairs . . . eight . . . seven
. . . not being concerned at all with how deeply you go
or how you go more deeply . . . six . . . easy . . .
comfortable . . . five . . . just allowing it to happen . . .
and four . . . comfortable and pleasant . . . three . . .
two . . . body relaxed yet your mind still aware . . .
one. . . .

And go in your mind to a special inner place of
deep relaxation and healing . . . an inner place of great
beauty, peacefulness, and security for you . . . a place
you have visited before, or one which simply occurs to
you now. . . .

It really doesn't matter where you go now in your
mind as long as the place is peaceful, beautiful, and

healing to you . . . take a few moments to look around this special inner place and notice what you see . . . what you hear . . . perhaps there's a fragrance or aroma here . . . and especially notice any feelings of peacefulness, safety, and connection that you feel here. . . .

As you explore, find the spot where you feel the most relaxed, centered, and connected in this place . . . become comfortable and quiet in this place. . . .

When you are ready, focus your attention on the symptom or problem that has been bothering you . . . simply put your attention on it while staying completely relaxed . . . allow an image to emerge for this symptom or problem . . . accept the image that comes, whether it makes sense or not . . . whether it is strange or familiar . . . whether you like it or not . . . just notice and accept the image that comes for now . . . let it become clearer and more vivid, and take some time to observe it carefully. . . .

In your imagination, you can explore this image from any angle, and from as close or far away as you like . . . carefully observe it from different perspectives . . . don't try to change it . . . just notice what draws your attention. . . .

What seems to be the matter in this image? . . . what is it that represents the problem? . . .

When you know this, let another image appear that represents the healing or resolution of this symptom or problem . . . again, simply allow it to arise spontaneously . . . allow it to become clearer and more vivid . . . carefully observe this image as well, from different perspectives . . . what is it about this image that represents healing? . . . .

Recall the first image and consider the two images

together . . . how do they seem to relate to each other as you observe them? . . . Which is larger? . . . Which is more powerful? . . . If the image of the problem seems more powerful, notice whether you can change that . . . imagine the image of healing becoming stronger, more powerful, more vivid . . . imagine it to be much bigger and much more powerful than the other. . . .

Imagine the image of the problem or symptom turning into the image of healing . . . watch the transformation . . . how does it seem to happen? . . . Is it sudden, like changing channels on television, or is it a gradual process? . . . If it is a process, notice how it happens . . . notice if what happens seems to relate to anything in your life. . . .

End your imagery session by focusing clearly and powerfully on this healing image . . . imagine it is taking place in your body at just the right place . . . notice whether you can feel or imagine any changing sensations as you imagine this healing taking place . . . let the sensations be sensations of healing . . . affirm to yourself that this is happening now, and that this healing continues in you whether you are waking . . . sleeping . . . imaging . . . or going about your daily activities. . . .

When you are ready, prepare to return to your waking consciousness . . . imagine yourself at the bottom of your imaginary staircase . . . and begin to ascend . . . one . . . two . . . allowing this image of healing to continue to work within you . . . three . . . becoming more and more aware of your surroundings . . . four . . . when you reach ten you may come wide-awake and alert, feeling refreshed and better than before . . . five . . . lighter and lighter . . . six . . . aware of the room you are in . . . seven . . . feeling refreshed and relaxed and better than before . . . eight . . . almost wide-awake now . . . nine . . . your eyes may want to open now . . . and ten . . . allow your eyes to open and come fully wide-awake . . . feeling refreshed, relaxed, and better than before . . . and stretch and smile and go about your day. . . .

Evaluating Your Experience

Take some time to write about and/or draw your experience. Describe the image of your problem in detail, and then the image of your healing. Were your images primarily physical and anatomical, or were they symbolic in some way? Notice your thoughts and associations with these images—if they remind you of something else in your life, make a note of that. Did any feelings come as you experienced this process? Did you feel any shift in feeling, sensation, or character of your symptoms from doing this imagery?

Using Drawings as Imagery

If you had trouble finding an image, it may help to doodle or draw your symptom, illness, or problem. Use crayons, oil pastels, colored pencils, felt pens, or any drawing material you have. Use big sheets of paper and just let your hand draw freely as you focus on your problem. Trust your instincts and let the drawing develop according to what feels right to you. Don't be concerned about the artistic quality of your creation—

the point here is to learn something, not create a work of art. You might even want to let your nondominant hand do the drawing. If there are words or a phrase that comes to mind as you draw, write them down somewhere on your drawing. When it seems complete, take some time to consider the way you have depicted your problem. What does it tell you? What seems to be the problem here?

When you feel you've learned what you can from this drawing, let yourself make another drawing that represents the process of healing. Let this drawing, too, emerge spontaneously—just follow out whatever wants to form. One patient of mine said, "I just let my hand please my vision, and I'm always surprised at what I end up with."

You may want to use these drawings to help you visualize more easily. Put them up where you will see them, and use them as a way to focus your attention when you begin your Healing Imagery sessions. If you found drawing helpful, you can use it to help you with any of the other imagery scripts in this book.

Working With Your Healing Imagery

When you imagine healing taking place within you, imagine it happening in the present. This may be difficult if you are feeling ill or are in pain, since the imagery may conflict with your experience. If you have a splitting headache, it may be hard to maintain a calm focus on an image of a cool, soothing stream washing your pain away. Stay relaxed and persevere. "Fake it till you make it." Think of Healing Imagery as an affirmation, a suggestion that will begin to lead you in the direction you desire. Even if you don't feel relief happening right away, be patient and consistent as you .imagine the healing process as vividly as you can. Your imagery can change more quickly and easily than your body. Physical healing, especially when you have a longstanding problem, may take some time.

How often should you do Healing Imagery? As often as you need to, if you have an intermittent symptom, and as often as you can if you're dealing with a chronic, difficult, or serious illness. No one knows the "dose-response" relationship of this technique yet, but it seems that people who really believe in imagery do it more often, more enthusiastically, and more carefully. They also get the best results. Relax and focus on your healing imagery as often and as clearly as you can. Even while you are going through your daily routines, you can close your eyes and briefly reaffirm your imagery. You may even find that you can do it without having to close your eyes.

Every time you focus on the image, it becomes stronger, and over a few weeks it becomes lodged in your unconscious mind. It's just like anything else that is new to you—like learning to play an instrument or a sport. At first it feels strange and unfamiliar, but as you do it more often, it becomes more comfortable and eventually it becomes unconscious, and you don't have to think about how you do it.

The Simontons have recommended fifteen minutes three times daily as a guideline for their cancer patients. For most medical problems, I encourage my patients to do Healing Imagery at least twice a day, ten to twenty minutes at a time, for several weeks. Don't forget, you may be working to replace an image of illness you have carried with you for months or years, and it may take some work.

You may begin improving as soon as you start doing Healing Imagery, or it may take some time to notice effects. If you have frequent symptoms, you should be able to notice some change within two weeks of regular practice. You may have dramatic relief, or it may be more subtle. Consider any benefit a sign that you are working in the right direction and continue your work.

If something you do in your imagery makes you feel worse, don't give up your efforts. If you can make yourself feel worse, you can probably make yourself feel better. Pay careful attention to the imagery that makes you feel worse. Imagine yourself doing the opposite of whatever you were imagining. When you find an image that brings feelings of improvement, stay with it.

If you are working on a problem that isn't accompanied by symptoms (such as many cancers), you may not be able to tell if the imagery is helping until your next medical evaluation. On the other hand, you may notice you feel refreshed, relaxed, more confident and optimistic after doing imagery, and that is encouraging and worthwhile in itself.

When I evaluate patients who want to use imagery this way, my first concern is to identify clearly the safe boundaries in which we can work. We identify the signs and symptoms that signal patients to call for a medical evaluation, and we select a period of time in which to evaluate their progress. You should do the same, determining a reasonable time for reevaluation in consultation with your doctor or other health professional. Try to give yourself a minimum of three weeks, and three months if you have a longstanding problem. Then reevaluate your condition and assess your progress.

If you have improved, continue working with your program. If not, experiment with your imagery and find an image that feels more powerful to you. Have you given it your best shot or is there more you could do? In either case, especially if you haven't improved, you may want to use the techniques in the next three chapters to improve your ability to support your own healing.

NOTES

1) Achterberg, J., and Lawlis, G. F. *Imagery of Cancer,* Institute for Personality and Ability Testing, Champaign, Illinois, 1978.

2) Pelletier, K., personal communication.

SEVEN

Meeting Your Inner Advisor

A Navy veteran talks with an imaginary old man called "The Helper" and learns how to rid himself of chronic asthma.

A female advertising executive follows the advice of a willowy young woman named Laura, whom she meets in her mind's eye. She puts full-spectrum lighting in her home and office and is greatly relieved of severe allergies.

An imaginary figure named Ricardo counsels a young psychiatrist, "You are a healer, but before you can heal others you must learn to heal yourself." Ricardo shows him a way to conduct therapy without the recurrent neck pain that has plagued him for months.

Spooky? Not really. Having a talk with an imaginary wise figure—an inner advisor—may sound strange, yet this is one of the most powerful techniques I know for helping you understand the relationships between your thoughts, your feelings, your actions, and your health.

We have much more information inside us than we commonly use. An inner advisor is a symbolic representation of that inner wisdom and experience. Your inner advisor should be thought of as a friendly guide to these valuable unconscious stores—an inner ally who can help you understand yourself more deeply.

Have you ever struggled with a problem and ultimately come to terms with it by listening to that "still, small voice within"? Do you pay attention to your gut feelings when you make important decisions? Or perhaps you have dreams that enlighten or guide you. Flashes of insight? Good hunches?

All of the above are ways you may be guided by something deep inside—a part of you usually hidden from conscious awareness. Imagining this guidance as a figure you can communicate with helps to make it more accessible.

Your inner advisor may offer advice in areas as diverse as nutrition, posture, exercise, environment, attitudes, emotions, and faith. Your advisor can serve as a liaison figure to that part of your mind that thinks in images and symbols; as an ambassador between the silent and verbal brains, the unconscious and conscious minds.

Let's look closely at the three people I mentioned at the beginning of this chapter. Frank, a twenty-eight-year-old ex-naval officer in Vietnam suffered with recurrent chronic asthma. This grew worse when he started a job as a rural deliveryman and had to pass hay fields and horses every day. Standard asthma medications only partially relieved his distress, and he didn't want to take steroid medications if there was any alternative. Testing confirmed strong allergies to both hay and horse dander. He didn't want to give up his job, which he both liked and needed, and was referred to me for help. With some skepticism, he agreed to explore his illness through imagery. As he relaxed and looked inside for an inner advisor, he saw an image of a stern older man working on a machine, who called himself "The Helper." The man reminded Frank of his grandfather, who had raised him on his farm.

In imagery, Frank saw himself as a small boy being punished by having to sweep out the horse barn, a job he hated. He saw himself beginning to wheeze while doing it and his grandfather telling him he didn't have to finish the job. Later, in his imagination, The Helper told him that now he was a grown man, and he could choose which jobs he was willing to do. He could refuse a job he didn't want without needing to get sick to get out of it. Hearing this, Frank felt relieved and his breathing improved. He was able to continue his route without asthma and has not had a recurrence in ten years.

The young woman executive, Justine, had allergies to many foods and chemicals. She, too, was reluctant to work with imagery, but finally became desperate enough to try. Laura, her advisor, when asked about her allergies, held out her hand and revealed a prism in her open palm. A single beam of white light entered the top of the prism and was refracted into a rainbow spectrum of light that radiated toward Justine. She asked Laura to explain what this meant and she answered, "You have light compression." She would say no more. Puzzled, I encouraged Justine to keep the image in mind throughout the week and meet with Laura again to see if she would clarify the message.

Some three days later, while looking through some old books, Justine came across a book a friend had given her months before: *Health and Light* by John Ott. Ott, the inventor of time-lapse photography, was also a pioneer in the field of photobiology, the effects of light on living organisms. In his book, he marshals evidence to support the view that full-spectrum sunlight is a nutrient needed for healthy human function. He believes that spending long days and nights in artificial lighting is a significant cause of illness in some people.

In a flash, Justine understood what Laura had been telling her. She went into her relaxed state and summoned Laura, who confirmed her discovery. With Laura's guidance, she devised a plan to correct the situation. She replaced all the light bulbs at home and in her office with full-spectrum bulbs, agreed to go outside in the sun for at least thirty minutes a day, and asked her boss for a desk near a window. Within two weeks, she reported herself almost completely free of allergies, and remained that way for eighteen months without further treatment.

The psychiatrist, Art, had recently completed his training and was working intensely in private practice. He began to experience severe pains in his neck, chest, and shoulders, especially when he was with his patients. As Art talked with his advisor, Ricardo, an image of himself in a suit of heavy armor appeared. The armor rested on his shoulders and chest. Ricardo told him the armor was there to protect him from his feelings, but it stood in the way of his being an effective therapist. He said the armor was made of "thinking and planning," and Art would need to discard it if he was to be of real help to his patients.

Inner Guidance: A Common Belief

Talking with an inner advisor is not a new idea. Most of the major philosophical, religious, and psychological traditions of mankind speak of inner guidance in one form or another. Many primitive cultures used rituals which included music, chanting, fasting, dancing, sacrifice, and psychoactive plants in order to invoke a vision that could inform and guide them at important times. Native American braves would go into the wilderness unarmed, without food and water, build a sweat lodge, and pray for contact with a guiding spirit. From such a visionary experience they would draw their names, their power, and their direction in life. The medicine man of the tribe might make a similar quest in search of healing for an ailing tribe member.

Catholic children are taught in catechism that they have a holy guardian angel who protects them and who can be called on in time of need. Many other religions teach a similar idea.

Children, whatever their religious or cultural background, often have imaginary playmates who talk with them, play with them, protect and support them in their imaginary play.

A surprising number of people tell me they "talk" to spouses or other loved ones who have died. In their talks they receive advice and comfort, as people do when they "talk" with their inner advisors.

All these experiences point to a common human notion—there is guidance available to us when we appeal to it, and when we are receptive to it. Meeting with an inner advisor is a way of making this intuitive guidance more available to you. Intuition is defined as the "power of knowing without recourse to reason" and is perceived by inner seeing, inner listening, and inner feeling. It may well be a specialized function of the right hemisphere. Through the right brain's ability to perceive subtle cues regarding feelings and connections, we are guided by what we call instincts, gut feelings, and hunches. By becoming quiet and attentive to our inner thoughts, we can use the talents of this neglected part of our minds most effectively.

It's not necessary to have any particular belief about the inner advisor in order to use it, but it's helpful for the technique to make sense to you one way or another. Whatever you believe—that the advisor is a spirit, a guardian angel, a messenger from God, a hallucination, a communication from your right brain to your left, or a symbolic representation of inner wisdom—is all right. The fact is, no one knows what it is with any certainty. We can each decide for ourselves. It can be reasonably explained psychologically, neurologically, theologically, metaphysically, or cybernetically, and none of these explanations is necessarily exclusive of any other. I'm satisfied that, for many people, the inner advisor is an effective way for them to learn more about their illnesses or issues, and the inner resources that can best help them move those situations toward healthy resolutions.

How Can an Inner Advisor Help Me?

First and foremost, an inner advisor can help you understand more about the nature of your illness, the part you play in it, and the part you might play in your own recovery.

Second, an inner advisor acts as a source of support and comfort; there is often a sense of peacefulness, of inner calm and compassion that stems from meetings with an advisor. In itself, this is often a real step toward healing, especially if you have been feeling depressed or panicky about your situation.

Claire, a therapist going through a very stressful divorce, supporting two children, and maintaining a busy professional life, had begun bleeding heavily between her periods. Medications had not controlled the bleeding, and she was set against having a hysterectomy. She broke down in tears as she met her inner advisor, overcome with the compassion she felt from this inner figure. The compassionate feeling allowed her to acknowledge how difficult her situation was and how well she was doing with it. Rather than engendering self-pity, this acknowledgment helped her struggle with and eventually come through her crisis with success, integrity, and an intact uterus, which stopped bleeding abnormally.

Third, working with an advisor can result in the direct relief of symptoms and recovery from illness. This usually comes as a result of realizing the function of a symptom and making changes so your body/mind no longer needs to create the symptom.

You may find it reassuring to know that while you do want to know what your advisor has to say, you don't have to do whatever it recommends. Whatever comes from your talk with your advisor, you will consider it carefully in the "clear light of day," and take a good look at what it might mean to act on that advice. You will evaluate the risks and benefits of following its advice and make your own decision about whether or not to follow it. The choices, and the responsibility, remain yours. Don't abandon your responsibility to your inner advisor, but consider what it has to tell you.

Testing the advisor is something you might want to do if it suggests a course of action that involves some risk for you. Let's say that your advisor tells you that you have to change your occupation in order to feel better. While this might be something you'd do if you *knew* it was really going to improve your health, you might be reluctant to make such a big change without some reassurance. Tell your advisor that you're considering the advice it's given you, and that it's difficult for you to imagine following it. Discuss your fears or concerns thoroughly, and let your advisor help you understand them more deeply and perhaps help you think of a way to change that takes your concerns into account. If, after you've explored the advice in depth, you still see significant risk, ask your advisor to give you a demonstration of its ability to help you get better.

I mentioned earlier that Dr. Irving Oyle first introduced me to the inner advisor technique. The first patient I remember him working with was a thirty-five-year-old jet-set entertainer named Eric who came to see Dr. Oyle with an unusual ankle problem. Once a month over the previous nine months, his left ankle had become swollen and very painful for four days. He had consulted three orthopedic surgeons, all of whom confirmed the swelling and inflammation in his ankle, but none of whom could make a diagnosis. X-rays of the ankle and laboratory tests on the ankle joint fluid showed no abnormality. Anti-inflammatory medications and injections provided no relief.

Eric was a very successful but driven entertainer who worked constantly, commonly flying halfway around the world on tours and frequently jetting back and forth from coast to coast. He more than loved his work, he was addicted to it—he had little else in his life. He was always working or planning new work, never took vacations, and had no outside interests or relationships. His tension level was palpable at a distance. He was enormously angry with his ankle because it rendered him unable to work four days a month.

Eric's inner advisor came in the form of a cartoonlike devil prodding him in the ankle with a pitchfork. It said there was more to life than work, and Eric had to begin experiencing his emotional side. To do that, he would have to start making room in his life for reflection, and his ankle was helping him do that. Eric was surprised at this message but felt it was "bullshit" and didn't see how it could be connected to his physical problem.

With Dr. Oyle's guidance, Eric struck a deal with his little devil, and agreed to take four days a month off to devote to rest, relaxation, and enjoyment. His inner advisor told him he would not have ankle pain again as long as he kept his bargain. For three months, Eric stuck to his agreement and had no pain or swelling. Feeling he was recovered, he skipped his days off the next month and the problem recurred with all its previous severity.

If you make a bargain with your advisor, make sure you *keep it*. Remember, you are dealing with a part of yourself here; you can't disrespect it without cost. Consider this a real relationship, and treat it with respect. Would you make an important business agreement and casually break it, or stand up a good friend for dinner? Why treat yourself with any less respect?

Robert, a fifty-two-year-old Jewish man with chronic abdominal pain and indigestion, had been diagnosed as having pancreatitis. His doctors had little to offer him but had urged him to follow a low-fat diet, which he had trouble doing. He found an inner advisor who called himself "Moishe." Robert said he looked like a cross between his brother, Morris, and the biblical figure Moses. Moishe, like the doctors, told Robert that he would feel better and give his pancreas a chance to recover if he followed a strict low-fat diet. Robert followed Moishe's advice for several weeks and felt better than he had in years. He then went on a trip, visiting his family, and forgot about his diet. Soon after a meal at a Chinese restaurant he had a severe episode of abdominal pain and vomiting. He tried to get back in touch with his advisor but had no success.

When he next came to visit me, I guided him through a relaxation process and politely asked Moishe to come and talk with Robert again. Moishe appeared in his imagery, but stood with his head turned away and wouldn't say anything. Robert asked him why he was silent, and he replied, "I don't have time to waste—if you're not going to be sincere about this, I am not going to talk to you." Robert apologized and committed himself again to working toward better health more conscientiously.

Today, two years later, Robert feels working with his inner advisor has been one of the most helpful things he has ever learned. Not only has Moishe helped Robert with his digestive problems, but he was also of great comfort during a very difficult six-month period in which Robert lost the two people closest to him. During that time, Moishe told Robert that he was only an intermediary figure who represented his connection with God. Robert said to me, "Why deal with a middle man?" and now, in his meditations, he feels a sense of inner connection to God. Sometimes he asks questions and receives answers; other times he just enjoys a deep sense of peacefulness.

If you make and keep your inner agreements, it's quite reasonable to ask for and receive some tangible evidence that what you are doing will pay off. If your advisor does have the ability to guide you toward healing, it should have the ability to let you know you are on the right path.

There may be times when your advisor may not be willing or able to give you immediate relief as a sign. If that's the case, ask it what needs to happen first before you can get some relief. This will often start you on the road that eventually leads to the relief you seek. Remember, testing is not the same as doubting. It's a request for evidence of fair value, and you must give fair value in return.

Should My Inner Advisor Appear in Any Particular Form?

Inner advisors often come as the classic "wise old man" or "wise old woman," but they come in many other forms as well. Sometimes they come in the form of a person you know, a friend or relative who has fulfilled this function for you in real life. These people may be living or dead, and it may be an emotional experience for you to encounter them in your inner world. Some people feel strange communicating with the figure of a deceased relative and wonder if this is really the spirit of the person they're talking with. If that's your belief, and you're comfortable with it, it can be a wonderful reconnection. Otherwise, it is enough to welcome it as a figure in your own mind that is wise and kind, and that has appeared in response to your request for help.

Advisors may also be animals or birds, plants, trees, even natural forces like the wind or the ocean. Sometimes people will encounter religious figures like Jesus, Moses, or Buddha, while others will find an angel, fairy, or leprechaun. Yoda from *Star Wars* often appeared as an advisor during the time the movie was playing, as did Obi Wan Kenobi. People sometimes encounter the advisor as a light or a translucent, ethereal spirit, and it's not uncommon to simply experience a sense of something calming, strong, and wise, without any visual image. Others communicate with an inner voice without any visual or feeling image.

Dr. David Bresler, head of the Bresler Medical Center in Santa Monica, California, frequently uses the inner advisor technique with people in chronic pain. His approach is somewhat different than mine, though the results seem quite similar. He guides people to relax in an imaginary quiet place, then asks them to get an image for a friendly creature that can act as their advisor. Many of his patients will get animal advisors such as Bambi the deer, or Chuckie the chipmunk. Dr. Bresler and I have compared notes at length and agree that people seem to be able to receive the same kind of information from the animal figures as from any other inner images of wisdom.

I explained this alternative once to a psychologist who had consulted me but was reluctant to get an inner advisor. As I described the cute little animal advisors many people created, he laughed and said he could see an image of a lion, looking at him and licking his chops. "Screw all those chipmunks," said the lion. "I'm here and I'm important." From this he understood that this inner part of himself was powerful and needed to be approached with respect.

Don't have expectations of any kind; they can stand in the way of your benefiting from the experience. If you are expecting a transcendent experience and a frog jumps into view, you might not recognize it as a potential inner advisor. The opposite may be equally true. Once, when Dr. Bresler and I were teaching a workshop for health professionals, we led the group through the guided imagery experience of meeting with an inner advisor. Afterward, one woman looked enormously frustrated. She was upset because all she ever experienced when she looked for an advisor was a "beautiful bright light that fills my whole body." We asked her how it felt to imagine herself filled with this light, and she said it was wonderful—it felt healing and energizing. But she was disappointed. She had been expecting a chipmunk!

The best way to work with this and any other imagery experience is just to let the figures be whatever they are. Welcome the advisor that comes and get to know it as it is. One advisor is no better than another, and there is no best way for them to communicate. People have learned profound lessons from gremlins named "Jack" and rabbits named "Thumper," as well as from more classical wisdom figures. Some advisors talk, others communicate their messages through their expressions or actions or by changing their forms completely. Sometimes people just "get the message" without really knowing how. A psychologist at one of our workshops wrote, "I don't *see* an advisor, and I don't *hear* anything, but *I do know what is being communicated.*" This is the essence of the inner dialogue, whether with an advisor or with other techniques you'll learn later.

It may take time to get to know your inner friend, to understand how it communicates, where it comes from, what it represents, and how best to make use of it. It's like a real relationship; treat it with respect, and you'll be pleasantly surprised at how useful it can be.

How Do I Meet My Inner Advisor?

Meeting your inner advisor is simple. The first step is to let yourself relax and go to your special inner place. When you're comfortable, quiet, and relaxed there, allow an image to appear for your inner advisor. Accept whatever image comes—whether it is familiar or not. Take some time to observe it carefully, and invite it to become comfortable with you, just as if it were real. After all, it is a *real* imaginary figure! Ask your advisor its name, and let it have a voice to answer you. You may hear the name in your mind or you may just understand its name—let yourself "play along" and accept whatever name comes to mind. It's important not to edit or second-guess the imagery at this stage. Take some time to become comfortable in the presence of your inner advisor, and as you grow more familiar with it, notice if it seems to be wise and kind. Notice how you feel in its presence. If it feels comfortable to you, ask your advisor if it would be willing to help you, and let it respond. If it is willing, tell it about your problem or illness and ask if it can tell you what you need to know or do to get

better. Let it answer you and stay open and receptive to
the answers that come.

Use the following script the same way you have
used the previous ones. This exploration will take
twenty-five to thirty minutes of uninterrupted time.

SCRIPT:

Meeting Your Inner Advisor

Begin to relax by taking a comfortable position,
loosening any restricting clothing, and making ar-
rangements for thirty minutes of unrestricted time . . .
take a few deep breaths and begin to let go of tension
as you release each breath . . . allow yourself a few
minutes to relax more deeply, allowing your body to
let go and your mind to become quiet and still. . . .
Imagine yourself descending the ten stairs that
take you deeper to your quiet inner place . . . 10 . . . 9
. . . deeper and more relaxed . . . 8 . . . 7 . . . easily and
naturally . . . 6 . . . 5 . . . deeper and more comfortably relaxed . . . 4 . . . your mind quiet and still, but
alert . . . 3 . . . 2 . . . deeper and more comfortably at
ease . . . and 1. . . .
As you relax more deeply, imagine yourself in
that special place of beauty and serenity you found as
you did the previous imagery exercises . . . take a few
minutes to experience the peacefulness and tranquility
you find in this place. . . .
When you are ready, invite your inner advisor to

join you in this special place . . . just allow an image to form that represents your inner advisor, a wise, kind figure who knows you well . . . let it appear in any way that comes and accept it as it is for now . . . it may come in many forms—a wise old man or woman, a friendly animal or bird, a ball of light, a friend or relative, a religious figure. You may not have a visual image at all, but a sense of peacefulness and kindness instead. . . .

Accept your advisor as it appears, as long as it seems wise, kind, and compassionate . . . you will be able to sense its caring for you and its wisdom . . . invite it to be comfortable there with you, and ask it its name . . . accept what comes . . . when you are ready, tell it about your problem . . . ask any questions you have concerning this situation . . . take all the time you need to do this. . . .

Now listen carefully to your advisor's response . . . as you would to a wise and respected teacher . . . you may imagine your advisor talking with you or you may simply have a direct sense of its message in some other way . . . allow it to communicate with you in whatever way seems natural. . . . If you are uncertain about the meaning of its advice or if there are other questions you want to ask, continue the conversation until you feel you have learned all you can at this time . . . ask questions, be open to the responses that come back, and consider them carefully. . . .

As you consider what your advisor has told you, imagine what your life would be like if you took the advice you have received and put it into action . . . do you see any problems or obstacles standing in the way of doing this? . . . If so, what are they, and how might

you deal with them in a healthy, constructive way? . . .
If you need some help here, ask your advisor, who is
still there with you. . . . When it seems right, thank
your advisor for meeting with you, and ask it to tell
you the easiest, surest method for getting back in touch
with it . . . realize that you can call another meeting
with your advisor whenever you feel the need. . . .

Say goodbye for now in whatever way seems
appropriate, and allow yourself to come back to
waking consciousness by walking up the stairs and
counting upwards from one to ten, as you have before.
When you reach ten, come wide-awake, refreshed and
alert, and remembering what was significant or important to you about this meeting. . . .

Evaluating Your Experience

When you open your eyes, take some time to write
down or record whatever happened in your experience.
If you met an inner advisor, describe it in detail. Did
you have a visual image or a sense of its presence, or did
answers come to your questions without any particular
image forming?

What did you ask your advisor, and what was your
advisor's response? Do you understand its response?
Are there other questions you would like to ask next
time you have this dialogue that would help clarify its
advice for you?

Did you learn anything useful from this experience? Is there any action you will take as a result of this
inner conversation, or is there something else that needs
to happen first?

Did you become aware of any obstacles to following your advisor's advice? If so, were you able to imagine constructive ways to deal with them?

Are there specific people who would be affected if you followed your advisor's recommendations? If so, how could you best address their concerns?

If you didn't meet an inner advisor, if your advisor was critical or hostile, or if you met more than one advisor, read the section of the next chapter that addresses your experience before taking the next step.

Discrimination and Inner Guidance

Evaluating the advice you receive is a critical aspect of working with an inner advisor. The advisor is one of many aspects of your unconscious mind, and it is possible for you to receive information from other inner sources. Weighing the potential benefits and risks of what's been suggested allows you to analyze what you've learned and discriminate between potentially useful and potentially risky actions.

Sometimes, however, the choices that offer the most benefits also involve the most risk. In medicine we use the concept of a risk/benefit ratio to help us decide among different treatments for an illness. The ideal treatment is, of course, completely safe and always effective, but unfortunately it has yet to be discovered. So we look for the ones that have the best ratio of safety to effectiveness, whether they be medicines, surgery, acupuncture, or psychotherapy. If a treatment is very safe and very effective, we use it more easily than one that is more dangerous and less effective. Or even more easily than one which is more dangerous yet more effective. This balance is a critical factor in evaluating treatment choices, one that you can apply in making your own choices.

Did your advisor suggest something that seems safe and offers potential benefit? Although you can't always tell in advance whether what's being suggested will be effective, you can usually evaluate its safety, and if it's safe, you can easily try it out to see if it works. For instance, your advisor might suggest that you relax more, or perhaps visualize something healing while you're relaxing. Here you are only risking fifteen to forty-five minutes a day for a few weeks to judge whether or not there is some positive effect.

There may be times, however, when the advisor suggests you do something more risky—like confronting someone or making a significant life change. You then need to weigh the potential benefit carefully before taking action. Assess your true beliefs about what is important to you, and make your choice from the most honest assessment you can make. You might also explore additional options through imagery and have further discussions with your inner advisor about the best and safest way to do what needs doing.

One of the most common fears people have is expressing themselves honestly to other people. We fear loss of love or respect, and we can easily ignore our own needs because of this fear. If the needs are important enough, they may find a means of expression in illness or symptoms.

Mary, twenty-four years old, had developed a sinus infection and was afraid that it would spread and get worse. She had had several similar infections earlier and always became extremely ill with them. Her treatment was complicated by her allergic reactions to every antibiotic usually prescribed for sinus infections. When encouraged to use imagery to explore the illness, she went to her quiet place and called on her inner advisor— a strong, loving older woman named Rose, who reminded her of the grandmother who raised her.

Mary asked about her illness and quickly became aware of the tension she'd been feeling between her and her husband during the previous two weeks. They were living under considerable financial pressure, and he had been working hard to organize a new business. He was tense, uncharacteristically edgy, and critical of her. He'd recently begun to have a couple of drinks after work, and this seemed to change his personality from an easygoing, loving one to a critical and angry one. Mary was frightened to talk to him about it for fear of making him even angrier. She valued her marriage highly and was afraid to do anything that might strain it. She realized all this in a flash. She had bottled up her own anger and fear, and Rose told her that was why she was sick. Mary asked Rose what to do, and Rose advised her to talk with her husband, quietly and lovingly, letting him know about her concerns when he wasn't tense and irritable.

After the imagery session, Mary was greatly relieved, both emotionally and physically. Subsequently, she had a good talk with her husband during a quiet evening and found him supportive and responsive. They were able to share their concerns and hopes again, and her recovery was complete within two days.

Mary's inner advisor helped her become aware of the feelings she was holding inside, the fear that kept them locked up, and a practical, loving way to express them and get the response she desired. By paying attention to her symptoms in this unusual way, she was able not only to recover from an illness, but to solve an even more serious problem in her life.

In the next chapter, I will address some of the common problems that occur as people begin to work with the inner advisor technique. If you had no problem with the inner advisor, you can now go to Chapter Nine, where you will learn another method of inner dialogue that can help you deepen your understanding of the meaning and purpose of your symptoms.

EIGHT

What to Do Until Your Advisor Comes and Other Common Problems

When people begin to work with the inner advisor technique, three problems surface frequently enough to merit special attention. The first is that no advisor appears; the second, that the inner advisor is hostile or critical; and the third is that there is more than one inner advisor. The sections that follow address these problems and the methods that have proven effective in their solution.

What If No Inner Advisor Appears?

If you didn't meet an advisor on the first try, be patient. Go to your quiet inner place regularly, relax there, and wait with a welcoming, inviting attitude until an image appears. If you do this once a day for a week, you'll find that your inner advisor will show up. Your advisor may turn out to be something that was there all

along, that you didn't recognize because you expected it
to be something else. Or it may be that you simply
haven't relaxed enough and are trying too hard. Working with imagery successfully is more a matter of
allowing than creating. Just wait in your inner place, as if
you were waiting for a bus. There's nothing you can do
to make it come sooner.

Relax more deeply and open yourself. This may in
itself stimulate your advisor's appearance. Remember
that the harder you try, the less likely you are to
succeed; the more deeply you relax, and the more
receptive you are to accepting whatever comes, the
more likely you are to have a good meeting with your
inner advisor.

I see many people who have spent years trying to
develop a backhand in tennis or learn to hit a golf ball
without a slice, who are disappointed and feel like
giving up when enlightenment doesn't come on the first
attempt. It's a skill to be able to relax and listen to your
inner mind—be patient and practice, and you'll be
successful.

Sometimes it helps to perform an imaginary ritual
while you wait. A nurse I know has a beautiful inner
place which contains a Japanese teahouse. When she
wants to meet with her advisor, she prepares tea in the
traditional Japanese way and waits for him. He always
shows up when the tea is ready. A business executive
patient of mine hikes through an imaginary wilderness
trail to a secret inner spot where he waits until nightfall
and builds a campfire. His advisor, an old Indian, appears to him when the fire is burning brightly. Other
people go to where their advisors "live"—in caves, on

mountaintops, even on other planets or other dimensions in their minds.

If you still aren't aware of receiving answers to your questions, here are some other ways to begin the process of dialogue with your inner wisdom:

1) *Imagine what your advisor would be like if you did have an advisor.* Would it be a man, woman, both, neither? Would it be human, spirit, animal, plant, other? What do you imagine it would look like? How would it move? How would it communicate with you? How would it feel to be with it and to talk with it about your problem? What do you think it would tell you about your problem? What might it ask you to do in order to begin helping yourself? How would you respond to its advice? When you've imagined in this way what your advisor would be like if you had one, close your eyes and go to your quiet place. Imagine that your would-be imaginary advisor is real and is there with you—let it communicate with you in the way you imagined it would. Let yourself pretend that you're having a talk with it about your problem—ask it questions, and imagine that it has a voice of its own and answers you. Just accept its answers for now as if they were real— whether they make sense or not, whether they are things you will do or not. Just remember what it says and indicates for you to do. Then open your eyes and write down what happened. Congratulations! You have an inner advisor!

2) *Draw or sculpt the ideal inner advisor.* Get some crayons or colored pencils and some big pieces of paper. Draw your ideal inner advisor. Don't worry about artistic merit—let yourself draw freely. You might pre-

fer to use modeling clay and sculpt your advisor. Just make one up till the "real one" comes along, and discuss your situation with it. Imagine what it would tell you if it were truly wise and cared about you.

3) *Imagine having a talk with a very good friend.* Imagine that you tell your friend, in detail, without holding anything back, about your illness, your thoughts, your feelings, and any questions you have that no one has been able to answer. Tell your friend everything you think is related, including things you've never told anyone before. Imagine your friend listening to you with compassion and responding to you—what does your friend say?

People often think about long-lost friends here, or even a dog or cat they were especially close to. If that happens to you, let yourself have an imaginary talk with your friend, dog, or cat, and let the figure respond to you in a way you can understand. Ask it if it will be your advisor, or if it can lead you to an inner advisor that can be of even more help.

Another variation of this approach is to imagine that your friend has the same problem you do, down to the smallest details. Imagine your friend telling you all about it and asking for your advice. What would you tell your friend?

4) *Think of a historical or mythological figure that fits your idea of what an inner advisor would be.* What would that figure say to you if it really knew you intimately and knew your problem and your questions? Imagine being in your quiet place with this figure (whether it is Winston Churchill, Merlin the Magician, Mother Teresa, Mahatma Gandhi, Eleanor Roosevelt, JFK, Venus de Milo, Jesus, or Willie Mays) and talking with

it about your situation. What does it say to you? What guidance, advice, or direction does it have for you? Notice the special qualities of this figure—are they qualities that might help you in your effort to get better?

5) *Write a letter to your wisest self.* Be clear and honest about your situation, your questions, your hopes, and your fears. Ask the questions that are most important to you. Then imagine that you are your wisest self and write yourself a letter back from this perspective. Respond to your initial letter, then correspond back and forth until you feel you have learned all you can about your situation and your options.

What If My Advisor Is Negative or Hostile?

Once in a while, a person imagines a character who's not kind and helpful but judgmental and punitive. Although you might learn something important from encountering and dealing with a hostile inner figure, this is *not* your inner advisor. An inner advisor is characterized by being both wise and caring. While your inner advisor may sometimes chide you or point out changes you need to make, its advice comes from a perspective of being helpful and compassionate, not coercive or blaming.

If the figure you perceive is heavily judgmental, listen carefully to what it says and how it expresses itself. You will probably notice familiar phrases and expressions—accusations and criticism you have heard before. This impostor advisor may be reminiscent of a parent or authority figure from your outer life. In psychoanalysis this is referred to as the "judgmental superego" and can be a very difficult inner figure to come to terms with. However, it can be one of the most important inner figures to learn to relate to effectively, since an internalized punitive authority figure can control and distort your life with its constant criticism. Belittling criticism can make you feel like a failure, no matter what you do, and can lead you to lose self-esteem, hope, purpose, and zest for life.

The simplest way to deal with this inner critic is to assert yourself. Tell it that you are in your quiet place to meet with your inner advisor, a loving, caring figure, and that in this special inner place you are in control. Let it know that you are looking for ways to become healthier and happier, and you'd be happy to listen to anything it has to say that would be constructive or helpful. Let it know that if it has concerns, you are willing to listen to them and will take them into account. But also let it know that you won't tolerate harping or criticism that doesn't lead toward growth and healing. Surprisingly, an inner critic will often change when addressed in this manner. It may express deep concerns underlying its behavior, often having to do with a desire to protect you and frustration at not being able to. If this happens, you can acknowledge the figure's good intentions and invite it to help you develop ways of living that keep you reasonably safe from harm yet open to growth, healing, and enjoyment of life.

If you have an active inner critic, learn to recognize its tone of voice and characteristic messages. Its inner messages tend to be repetitive and become quite recognizable once you start paying attention to them. Typically, they say things like, "This will never work" or

"There, see? You didn't get an inner advisor—you're no better at this than you are at anything else." However the inner critic phrases it, its basic message is "You're not good enough."

Cognitive therapists help people become aware of negative inner messages by having them write them down as they occur. Then a new thought is chosen to replace each habitual self-suggestion. When the person notices himself thinking or repeating his old thought, he stops, mentally "cancels" the thought, and consciously replaces it with the new, self-affirming thought. Over time, the negative thoughts come less frequently, and the positive ones begin to come more easily.

Recognizing and standing up to an inner critic is important because the self-image it generates often becomes a self-fulfilling prophesy. If you feel worthless, you will treat yourself as if you were worthless, and it will show in the choices that shape your health. The opposite is also true—dealing with an inner critic consciously and effectively can be extremely therapeutic.

Iris, a twenty-six-year-old undergraduate, wanted to lose weight. Whenever she went on a diet, however, she suffered severe periods of anxiety and depression. Her initial advisor was a witch who looked "something like the Wicked Witch of the West and something like my mother." Iris had a difficult relationship with her mother, whom she described as overbearing, hypercritical, and interfering. Many years of psychotherapy had made little difference in her ability to relate to her mother effectively. She yearned to be close to her mother, yet ended up in tears and rage almost every time they talked.

The inner witch figure was deprecating and skeptical of Iris's ability to lose weight. She laughed when we asked her to help. Many attempts were made to enlist the witch's aid and to find out what she had to offer. She persisted in belittling Iris and undermining every attempt she made to help herself. She was critical of everything Iris was doing and offered no constructive advice.

Finally I asked Iris what she wanted to do with the witch. She responded by imagining herself pouring water all over the witch and watching the witch dissolve, just like in *The Wizard of Oz*. She felt unusually calm and relieved as she considered the pool on the floor. She now felt she had some power over the witch, and experienced a sense of freedom that was unusual for her.

Over the next few weeks, Iris was able to recognize the witch when she heard thoughts in her head reminiscent of the witch's negativism. When she did, she would focus on the image of dissolving the witch and would have a "good feeling" every time she did it. As time went on, some unanticipated changes occurred: the witch in her imagery turned into a matronly figure who eventually became her friend. In their discussions, the witch told Iris that she had originally been a good witch but had an "evil spell" put on her a long time ago. Iris related this to her mother's upbringing by her grandmother, who was mentally disturbed. Iris found herself more understanding of her mother and much more able to relate to her without losing her temper and feeling resentful. She also succeeded in losing the weight she had set out to lose.

It's difficult to banish an important figure like an inner critic entirely, and it may not even be in your best

interest. You can, however, order it aside temporarily while you establish a working relationship with a friendly, supportive inner advisor who can become a strong ally. After you have done this, you will be more familiar with the process of inner dialogue, and your advisor can help you deal with your inner critic effectively.

Occasionally, an inner advisor will appear as a frightening, although not necessarily critical, figure. While this is unusual, I recommend you attempt to befriend the figure, whatever it is. The image is there for a reason—your inner mind created it in response to your question. It may represent the thing you most need to confront and grapple with in order to improve and may also be the thing you least want to deal with.

While the figure may scare you, there are ways to render it more approachable in imagery. You can imagine that you are protected by a force field or by a magic cape that surrounds you and renders you invisible and undetectable. You can observe the figure from this safe place and begin to understand what it might represent and how best to deal with it. You can also have a magic ring that radiates powerful light rays that transform monsters into friendly figures. This will often give you an idea of the positive side of what the image represents. You can have a laser sword or any kind of protective device or shield that can allow you to deal with the image safely. It's often interesting to notice what the shield is made of and what its qualities are—these may be qualities in yourself that will help you deal with this issue most productively. Finally, remember it's *your* imagination—you can "dematerialize" a figure by opening your eyes.

The idea is to create for yourself an inner condition which allows you to get to know and come to terms with whatever has shown up in your inner landscape in response to your questions. Whatever it is, it's *your image*. If it's frightening, it's *your fear;* if it angers you, it's *your anger;* if it makes you sad, it's *your sadness.* In imagery you have an opportunity to deal with these important, perhaps controlling aspects of your life. You can work with them where they have their effects on you—in your own mind and heart. The challenge and opportunity are to summon the inner resources to deal with these issues, thoughts, and feelings so that you are no longer controlled by them. In mythology, this is the hero's journey, and it is the quest we each must undertake in the search for healing.

If you find yourself unable to deal with a negative figure with the approaches mentioned above, you may want to enlist the help of a professional skilled with guided imagery. The most difficult issues to deal with are often the most important ones, and a good guide can help you explore areas where you don't feel confident.

What If More Than One Advisor Appears?

It's not uncommon for people to have more than one inner advisor turn up, especially after using imagery for a while. Some people have whole communities of inner advisors, each with a different gift: a wise teacher who provides advice, guidance, and clear thinking; a wise woman who provides compassion, understanding, and a sense of loving; a child who teaches playfulness and trust. If your advisor is unable to help you, ask it to "refer" you to another inner figure who knows more about the issue at hand. Another figure will emerge, often with new qualities, more information, and a different perspective. Like people, advisors may have specialized areas of expertise. One patient of mine, a school teacher, has five advisors that he meets with in his quiet place. They are all relatives of his; some are living, some are not. When he has a question he needs help with, he goes to his quiet place and asks the advisor or advisors who know the most about his problem to step forward and help him understand it.

Your whole inner mind is an "advisor" because it contains a vast amount of information about you and your well-being. It will naturally try to express those thoughts, feelings, and actions that are most important in your life. When you ask for an image of something, whether it's a symptom, an illness, a problem, or a feeling, the image will give you information about that "something" which you may not have been aware of. So, if you feel like it, you can let your advisor change forms or let yourself use many different images as advisors. On the other hand, if you have one advisor who works well for you, stick with it and have it guide you through the learning process that needs to happen.

Your inner advisor is a friendly guide to your inner life. With its assistance, you may want to explore your illness and your potential for healing even more deeply. Working directly with your symptoms in imagery will allow you to do that, and you can learn how by reading the next chapter.

NINE

Listening to Your Symptoms

Your inner advisor may have told you what you need to know about your symptoms or illness and how to go about resolving the problem. If so, you may not need to use the technique in this chapter, which begins a dialogue with an image that represents your symptom. If you need to know more, however, or if you are for any reason uncomfortable with the idea of an inner advisor, this exploration will be worthwhile. In a sense, you will be "eliminating the middle man," and attending directly to the source of the problem. You can use receptive imagery to help you understand the purpose of the symptom and what it will take to allow healing to proceed.

In this chapter, I will expand on the idea of a symptom as feedback, describe the most common meanings and functions of symptoms, discuss some concerns and precautions about using imagery to explore your symptoms, and give you a script that will lead you through an imaginary dialogue with your symptoms.

While symptoms are usually unpleasant, they are not the "enemy." In fact, they serve as a natural warning system that, seen in the right perspective, can help keep you in the best possible health. Symptoms are like warning lights or gauges in your car. When the oil light goes on in your car, would you take it to the closest gas station and ask the mechanic to rip out the light? Or tape over it so you can go about your business? Then why go to the doctor looking only for relief of symptoms? You may miss a warning that can prevent a future catastrophe.

Careful histories of people who come down with serious illnesses almost always reveal earlier warning signs that were ignored or treated superficially. Doctors commonly see patients who have treated their stomach pain for years with medications—palliating, tolerating, or ignoring the signal that something is out of balance until something more serious, like a heart attack, brings the message home.

Unfortunately, we are not usually taught that our bodies are intelligent and can communicate with us. We are disconnected from our body language, as we are from our emotions. We have somehow given away our birthright in the area of health and healing. We have come to assume that, yes, a symptom is a message—but all it says is "Go see your doctor"!

What would it be like if you were able to understand your symptoms and use the self-healing intelligence of your body, your feelings, and your spirit? Why not ask yourself what you need and be receptive to the answers that come from deep within? Is it so strange, after all, to think that the intelligence that created your body in the first place would be able to let you know what it needed in order to be healthy? Whatever created your body—whether you call it God, nature, life, genes, or DNA—was smart enough to make your head. If it can make your head, why not a headache? And if it can make a headache, why not a thought that can tell you what the headache means?

The Common Meanings and Functions of Illness

Illnesses may simultaneously express a person's distress and represent an attempt to relieve that distress. It is often useful to consider any benefits an illness may bring as a means of understanding its possible function. In *Getting Well Again*, (J. P. Tarcher, Los Angeles, 1978), the Simonton group describes the five most common benefits their cancer patients listed when they were asked to identify positive things about having cancer. These are: (1) Having permission to get out of dealing with troublesome situations or problems; (2) receiving attention, care, and nurturing from others; (3) having the opportunity to regroup psychologically to deal with a problem or find a new perspective; (4) finding incentive for personal growth or for modifying undesirable habits; (5) not having to meet the high expectations of themselves or others.

Whether these factors play a role in the formation of cancer is unknown, but they are certainly important in the development of many other common illnesses. Further, even if they are not causative, benefits derived secondarily from illness may interfere with your motivation to recover. Identifying the possible advantages of having your symptoms or illness lets you begin developing healthier ways to accomplish the same objectives.

At worst, if you recognize any benefits that come with being ill, you can make the best use of them. Other potential benefits of illness have been identified by many clinical observers. Gerald Edelstein, M.D., is a psychiatrist and hypnotherapist in the San Francisco Bay area. In his book *Trauma, Trance, and Transformation,* he reviews and paraphrases the work of another well-known psychotherapist, Leslie LeCron, who suggested that there were seven common unconscious reasons for the development of symptoms. These are:

1) The symptom may be a symbolic physical expression of feelings you are otherwise unable to express. This can be called "organ language"—a broken heart, a pain in the neck, not being able to stomach something, getting cold feet, feeling weak in the knees, putting something behind you, and so on.

2) The symptom may be the result of an unconscious acceptance of an idea or image implanted earlier in life. Thus, the message "you're a bad girl, and no one worthwhile could ever love you" repeated often or under particularly emotional circumstances could result in poor self-image, depression, self-destructive behavior, and difficulty in relationships later in life. In a real sense, we are all hypnotized as children. We look to our parents, and later to teachers and peers, to define our sense of self. The images we form of ourselves in these early years often form the unconscious basis for patterns of feelings, behavior, and physiology later in life.

3) The symptom may result from traumatic past experiences that have been highly emotional and then generalized. Edelstein feels that such experiences are

often at the base of phobias. Someone badly frightened by a dog, for example, may expect all encounters with dogs to be similarly bad. While these symptoms tend to be behavioral or psychological, they may also manifest physically, as in the case of the asthmatic deliveryman discussed in Chapter Seven.

4) The symptom provides benefits or solves a problem, as the Simonton list indicates. If so, the focus needs to be on ways to enjoy the benefits without having to be sick.

5) A symptom may be the result of an unconscious identification with an important, beloved person in your life. The "anniversary illness" is a well-known phenomenon in medicine. People may fall sick on or near the anniversary date of someone's death. Frequently, the symptom is similar to the symptoms the deceased person experienced. The identification may also be with people still living, or with historical or fictional roles. One patient of mine with cancer was shocked to find through her imagery that, as a child, she had always imagined herself as an actress playing roles where the heroine dies a tragic, dramatic death. She was struck by the similarity to feelings she was experiencing about her current illness and its effects on the people around her, and began imagining herself instead as a heroine who overcame and survived adversity.

6) A symptom is often a manifestation of an inner conflict. There may be an unmet need or desire that is forbidden by family, friends, society, or one's own inner judgments. The symptom may prevent you from carrying out a forbidden action, or may allow you to fulfill the desire symbolically. Sometimes it does both at once.

A priest I once saw as a patient had an extremely painful, immobile right shoulder. It prevented him from using his right arm and had not responded to extensive conventional treatment. He said it was so painful that he wasn't able to carry out his responsibilities as a priest and had asked his superior for a sabbatical leave. In an imagery session he saw himself angry, righteous, and carrying a placard in his upraised right arm. The anger and placard spoke directly to grievances he had with the church bureaucracy, but hadn't been able to express effectively. As he began to share these feelings, he saw how his painful shoulder simultaneously allowed him to stop doing work he didn't believe in and express his pain and anger to his organization. He also saw, however, that the message was disguised, unclear, and less effective than it would be if he were to articulate it openly. He realized the need for him to come to terms with the issues involved. Over the weeks that followed, he was able to clarify his own values and bring his grievances to the proper authorities. His physical healing paralleled his psychological and emotional healing in an almost linear manner.

7) Symptoms may be a result of an unconscious need for self-punishment. This often results from the "childhood hypnosis" mentioned in the second dynamic above, where you have unconsciously accepted a message that you are bad and need to be punished. It may also be an unconscious attempt to atone for a traumatic event for which you feel responsible, or an attempt to prevent something from happening again. Children often feel they are to blame for their parents' unhappiness, illnesses, alcoholism, or divorces. They may carry this unconscious sense of guilt until it is unearthed and

worked through. Disguised and under the surface, it may manifest in many ways in their lives—as physical pain, illness, failed relationships, or underachieving.

There may be more than one reason at work in the formation of a particular symptom. When you explore your own imagery, any of the above dynamics may become apparent, or there may be other needs or functions represented by your symptoms. For now, notice whether any memories, images, or strong emotions were triggered by any of the dynamics mentioned above. They may be helpful clues as you continue to explore the personal meaning of your symptoms.

The Saving Grace of Illness— A Personal Experience

The first time I was aware of the possible benefits of an illness was when I was at the University of Michigan Medical School. I had just started my three-month rotation on pediatrics, and had been assigned to the university hospital ward where the sickest children were treated. As we made rounds with the chief resident, he told us each child's history, both medical and personal. I felt increasingly depressed as I heard the stories of these small children with serious illnesses. I had at that time very little awareness of my own emotions. I was learning to be a doctor, and in the 1960s medical students and doctors I knew didn't talk about their feelings in the face of illness. Then, a remarkable thing happened. As we sat around the conference table after rounds, the chief resident put his head in his hands and began to cry. His crying turned into deep sobbing, and through his tears he was saying, "I can't take it anymore . . . I can't stand to see one more kid die. . . ." The attending staff physician told us to go home for the day as he moved to comfort the chief. The next day, the chief resident quit. The day after, I developed severe nausea, a fever, and extreme weakness.

I underwent the kind of medical workup that is only possible in a university medical center. My liver was enlarged, and my liver enzymes were abnormal, but everything else was normal. I had some type of hepatitis (the cause never was identified) and was not allowed to return to the wards until my lab tests were normal. I was very ill for a few days, then moderately ill for a few days, and felt fairly well after that, though I tired easily. My liver function tests remained elevated, however, for two and a half months. I had my first normal lab panel the weekend my pediatrics rotation ended.

While I never thought at the time that I got sick because of my pediatrics experience, I was aware that, after the first few days when I was really sick, I was grateful not to have to go back to the wards. If I consider this illness in light of the functions I have reviewed, I can see that it relieved me from a responsibility I didn't want to have, and it gave me time to think a great deal about whether or not I wanted to continue in medicine. To some extent I imagine I identified with the chief resident, whose feelings and honesty I admired. Looking back, I have no doubt that this illness served an important function for me.

It is often easier to see the benefits of illness in retrospect. It may be useful to you to review previous experiences you've had with illness before exploring

what is happening now. Dennis Jaffe, Ph.D., a noted
health psychologist and author of *Healing From Within,*
offers a helpful way to do this. Dr. Jaffe recommends
you take a large sheet of paper and draw a timeline
across the bottom, with marks for five-year periods.
Above this line, mark important health events in your
life—serious illnesses, recurrent health problems, and
accidents. Above that, note the important events and
changes in your life during those periods. Notice if there
seems to be any correlation between stressful events, or
clusters of change, and your health.

Be open, receptive, and nonjudgmental as you
consider illness from this perspective. Few people
would ever choose illness consciously for *any* of the
reasons I've presented in this chapter. Your purpose is to
discover what your *unconscious* response may have been
to a difficult situation, so that you can more consciously
play a role in your recovery. When you discover the
purpose of your symptom, you have a chance to develop ways to fulfill that purpose that may not require
you to be ill at all.

Using Imagery to Explore Your Symptoms

While you may have found the previous consider-
ations useful, they are essentially "left-brain" methods
of analyzing the meaning of your illness. A simpler,
more direct way to understand your symptom is to
relax, focus your attention on it, allow an image to
come to mind that can represent the symptom (as you
did in Chapter Five), and then have an imaginary conversation with it. Ask it why it's there, what it wants

from you, what it needs from you, and *what it's trying to do for* you. A script will follow later that will guide you through this process in detail.

As you begin to work with imagery this way, several points need to be addressed. One of these is the difference between a diagnosis and the personal meaning of your illness.

I have already discussed the necessity of making sure you have a clear understanding of your medical condition and the options you have for treatment. While no one should be forced to have medical treatment, I believe you deserve the best possible assessment of what conventional medicine has to offer. Once you understand your condition on that level, however, you need to explore the *personal* meaning of your symptoms. To do this, you must temporarily *put aside the diagnosis you have been given.*

Most people, doctors included, don't realize that a diagnosis is not a "real" thing. A diagnosis is the way we classify a certain pattern of findings in a given system of medicine. Patients with the same symptoms and signs of illness will have different diagnoses depending on when and where they live and the systems of medicine practiced there.

For instance, a patient with vertigo and ringing in the ears may be diagnosed as having "Ménière's syndrome" by a Western physician. A practitioner of traditional Chinese medicine, however, might diagnose the same patient as having "Yang Fire of the Liver Rising." In another culture, a shaman might diagnose that an evil spirit has entered the sufferer's head. To most of us, the Western doctor's diagnosis sounds the most authoritative and scientific, until we look closely at what it

means. Ménière's syndrome is defined as "A syndrome
believed to be caused by some derangement of the inner
ear, characterized by hearing loss, tinnitus, and vertigo,
which may be severe and chronic." In other words, by
diagnosing your problem as Ménière's syndrome, your
doctor is telling you that you have ringing in the ears
and dizziness. The diagnosis is simply a label.

In this instance, as in many others, our medical
system of classification fails to meet the two most
important criteria of a diagnosis, as seen from the
standpoint of the patient. It neither clarifies the nature of
the problem, nor does it lead to an effective remedy.
This is why it is important to realize that a diagnosis is a
name, not a sentence to a particular outcome.

People have widely varying reactions to most illnesses and to most treatments. While there is an "aver-
age" or "typical" course, there are almost invariably
exceptions which are important to know about. You
should learn about the typical course of your illness, but
also ask your doctor about exceptional patients he or she
has known. Do some people do better than others?
What seems to make the difference? If you have a
serious illness, has anyone ever recovered from it?
What's the best possible course of the illness? Will your
doctor be willing to support your efforts to recover, or
does he or she think they are "unrealistic"?

Hope is very important to healing, and there is a
difference between hope and false expectations. A patient of mine with breast cancer told her radiation
oncologist that she had great faith in him and felt that he
was going to help her overcome her cancer. He told her
that he would do his best but didn't want her to get her
hopes up. Shocked, she told him, "Doctor, I'm doing

everything I can to get my hopes up! Without hope, what do I have?" As Dr. Bernard Siegel, a cancer surgeon at Yale, says, "In the absence of certainty, there is nothing wrong with hope."

The point is, diagnosis is important so you can assess your medical treatment options. When you use imagery to explore your symptoms, however, focus on your symptoms as you experience them and temporarily set aside what you have been told about your illness. If you have back and leg pain, and it has been diagnosed as coming from a herniated disc, use the pain, not the disc, as the focus of your investigation. If you have an illness without symptoms, then focus on the involved area of your body.

Anxiety and Resistance

A second concern about using imagery to explore your symptoms is the fear you may have of encountering something traumatic. While this is possible, it seems to be quite rare in the self-care setting. Several thousand people have used my self-care imagery tapes over the past five years without reporting a single such problem. Emmet Miller, M.D., a physician in Menlo Park, California, has produced an excellent series of relaxation, self-hypnosis, and guided imagery tapes. With tens of thousands of his tapes sold over more than ten years, he has yet to hear of such a problem. Psychological defenses against remembering traumatic events are generally quite effective, and the most sophisticated therapeutic attempts to work through them are often frustrated. If a really traumatic insight were to burst through from using these methods, I would assume that it was just below the surface and would have soon become apparent. Nevertheless, by using imagery this way, you are inviting your unconscious to tell you what's going on inside, and it may well do just that. You need to cultivate an attitude that allows you to look at what comes back and explore its meaning without judgment or fear.

If you feel anxious as you consider the kind of self-exploration I am suggesting, pay attention to your fear. How strong is it? Is it mild anxiety or a feeling of excitement that comes when you venture into a new area? Or do you become really tense, have trouble breathing, get headaches, and experience worrisome levels of fear? If you experience a lot of anxiety, you are probably better off exploring this area with qualified professional help.

One common reason for anxiety at this point is the fear that your symptom may ask you to give up the thing that is closest to your heart, or hardest to let go of. Sometimes it will, but often it won't. If this is your concern, remember two things. First, *you do not have to do what you imagine your symptom wants you to do*. Instead, you will weigh the benefits against the risks and look for the safest, easiest way to use what you have learned from your illness to symptom. You *always* have the choice of doing nothing and maintaining your position as it is. Second, while healing sometimes requires difficult changes, it doesn't always. You may be surprised to find that what is called for has little or nothing to do with what you feared. Your symptom's need may be easier to satisfy than you ever imagined, and may bring you benefits beyond your expectations.

Anne, a thirty-five-year-old writer, had experienced eight months of recurrent respiratory and intestinal infections and was frustrated with the repeated rounds of doctors' visits and antibiotics that brought her short-term relief but no improvement in her general health. As we discussed her life, she revealed that she was unhappy about certain aspects of her marriage though she didn't want to leave it. She was terrified that her illness signaled a need to break away from her husband.

We began to work with imagery, and after several sessions I asked her to allow an image to form that represented something she could do to help herself regain her good health. An image of a large beautiful oak tree appeared. It was strong, old, stable, and calming. As she sat beneath this tree, she felt calm and protected. Then she experienced an urge to climb the tree. As she reached the top, she found she could comfortably sit in its branches and enjoy a "vast overview" of her world. She felt it indicated that she needed to use her inner strength and wisdom to get a better perspective on what was important to her in life.

Over the next few weeks, as she looked at various aspects of her life from this high perch, she realized that her love for her mate was still strong, but needed to be nourished. She saw how she had become buried in worries about money and her writing, which had been sporadic and unproductive. She took steps to renew the warmth in her relationship and found her husband quite happy to have her attention again.

Anne was also surprised and pleased to find herself inspired with creative ideas for writing as she relaxed in her "crow's nest." Two months after beginning to work with imagery she told me that she not only was fully recovered, but was writing productively and felt better than she had in years. She was amazed and pleased to see that out of her attention to her illness had come not only physical healing, but the restoration of both her relationship and her creativity.

If, like Anne, you have more than a little anxiety as you consider exploring your symptoms, it may be best to explore those feelings before moving on. I believe in respecting fear, in treating it as we treat a symptom— not as an enemy, but as a signal that something needs to be considered before taking another step. If this feels right to you, please skip to Chapter Eleven now. It will help you clarify your fears and take a look at how best to deal with them as you explore.

Imagery Is Not Just Wishful Thinking

Another common concern about imagery is that it may just be indulging in wishful thinking. By imagining your fondest dream coming true, by seeing your hopes manifest in imagery, you may risk being unrealistic and being led down a primrose path. This, of course, is certainly possible. Your hopes and fears both exist in your imagination along with your "realistic" images of life. If you know that, you are unlikely to be led astray. As always, discrimination is needed. If your imagery of how to go about healing seems "too good to be true," you may need to test it, as you may have tested the information you received from your inner advisor.

Though I have described testing of imagery information before, it is an important enough process to merit a second discussion. To test a vision that seems far-fetched or unrealistic, ask yourself the following questions: What is required of me to have this vision come true? How will I know if it's coming true? Is there any way to track my progress objectively? If I follow the lead of this imagery, what am I risking? Are there safeguards I can establish that can protect me or minimize my risk as I test it? Is the risk acceptable, considering the potential gain? Can I bear the loss if it doesn't work?

There are times, of course, when it's just not possible to proceed with absolute safety. Life is a risky business, and there are no guarantees in any kind of medicine or healing. The most sensible approach is not to take *unnecessary* risks, minimize those you do take, and look carefully at the relative potential for benefits.

As you begin to work with the imagery process that follows, you may become aware of negative feelings toward your symptom or illness. These are perfectly natural. They hurt you, frighten you, limit you, and interfere with your life. As you encounter an image that represents your symptoms, you may notice similar feelings arising. Expressing your feelings to the image, then letting it respond, may be the beginning of better understanding, as you will see when you practice the exercise in this chapter.

How to Listen to Your Symptoms

I am indebted to Dr. Naomi Remen for developing the larger part of the script included in this chapter. Dr. Remen originally recorded this script as part of our self-care tape series. In her introduction to this tape, she explains, "If you have a chronic illness, you already have a relationship with it. That relationship is often not the best it could be and may be characterized by mistrust, hostility, and fear. Dialoging with the symptom or with an image that represents it opens up lines of communication that may have been closed, and may lead to an improvement in the relationship. This improvement is often experienced as a decrease in pain, anxiety, or depression, and in some cases, as improvement in the illness itself."

Expressing your feelings in imagery can be the beginning of a dialogue, and it is possible to express anger, fear, or sadness, yet allow communication to continue. Take the attitude of a good negotiator or arbitrator. Find out what the "opposing" party wants, what it needs, what it will take, and what it has to offer if its needs are met. This is the essence of the inner dialogue process, and an attitude free of judgment will facilitate this conversation. In diplomatic circles it is said "There is no good and bad, only opposing views of the good." A diplomatic attitude in your imagery exploration may lead to inner peace, where before there was only conflict. Your goal is relief of the symptom or healing of the illness, but your approach will be negotiation rather than warfare.

As you work with the following imagery process, allow yourself to relax and accept what comes to mind. Let the images you encounter speak for themselves, and consider what comes to you carefully. Give yourself room to explore by maintaining a nonjudgmental, curious attitude. Approach this as an investigation, a consideration of your problem in a broader perspective.

When you are through with the process that follows, you will, as always, reflect on, weigh, and analyze whether what you learned is relevant or important to act on.

By now, you know to take a comfortable position, make sure you will not be interrupted for about thirty minutes, and either have a friend read the following script, make a recording of it, or work with our prerecorded tape.

SCRIPT:

Listening to Your Symptoms

Begin as always by taking a comfortable position, loosening any tight clothing, . . . have some writing paper and a pen or pencil close at hand. . . .

Take a couple of deep, slow breaths, and let the out breath be a real "letting go" kind of breath . . . imagine that any unnecessary tension or discomfort begins to flow out of your body with each exhalation . . . then let your breathing take its own natural rate and rhythm, allowing yourself to sink a little deeper and become more comfortable with each gentle breath. : . .

Invite your feet to release and relax any tension that may be there . . . notice them beginning to let go . . . invite your calves and shins to release as well . . . your thighs and hamstrings . . . your pelvis, genitals, and hips . . . feel your whole lower body releasing and relaxing as it has so many times before . . . just allow-

ing your body to head for a deeper, more comfortably
relaxed and focused state . . . and as your body relaxes,
your mind can become quiet and still as well . . . easily
and naturally . . . without effort. . . .

Allow your low back and buttocks to join in the
releasing and relaxing . . . allowing these large muscles
to become loose and soft and take a well-deserved
break . . . allow your abdomen to relax as well . . . the
muscles of your abdomen, flanks, and midback relaxing more deeply . . . the organs in your abdomen as
well . . . your chest muscles . . . your shoulder blades
and in between your shoulder blades . . . letting go . . .
easily . . . naturally . . . the organs in your chest . . .
your shoulders letting go . . . your neck muscles . . .
your arms . . . forearms . . . wrists . . . hands . . .
fingers . . . and thumbs . . . releasing and relaxing . . .
comfortably and easily . . . releasing your scalp . . .
forehead . . . face . . . and jaws . . . the little muscles
around your eyes. . . .

And to relax more deeply . . . to become quiet in
mind and body . . . imagine yourself in that special,
quiet inner place you've visited before . . . a special
inner place of peacefulness . . . serenity . . . and security for you . . . take a few moments to look around
and notice what you see there . . . and what you hear
in this special place . . . and any odor or aroma . . . and
especially the feelings of peacefulness and safety that
you feel here . . . and find the spot in which you are
most comfortable . . . and become centered and quiet
in that spot. . . .

When you are ready, direct your attention to the
symptom or problem that has been bothering you . . .
your symptom may be a pain, weakness, or dysfunc-

tion in some part of your body or a mood or emotions
that are uncomfortable for you . . . as you focus on the
sensations involved, allow an image to appear that
represents this symptom . . . simply allow the image to
appear spontaneously, and welcome whatever image
comes—it may or may not make immediate sense to
you . . . just accept whatever comes for now. . . .

Take some time just to observe whatever image
appears as carefully as you can . . . if you would like it
to be clearer, imagine you have a set of controls like
you do for your TV set, and you can dial the image
brighter or more vivid . . . notice details about the
image . . . what is its shape? . . . color? . . . texture?
. . . density? . . . How big is it? . . . How big is it in
relation to you? . . . Just observe it carefully without
trying to change it in any way . . . How close or far
away does it seem? . . . What is it doing? . . .

Just give it your undivided attention . . . as you do
this, notice any feelings that come up, and allow them
to be there . . . look deeper . . . are there any other
feelings present as you observe this image? . . . When
you are sure of your feelings, tell the image how you
feel about it—speak directly and honestly to it (you
may choose to talk out loud or express yourself si-
lently). . . .

Then, in your imagination, give the image a
voice, and allow it to answer you . . . listen carefully to
what it says . . .

Ask the image what it wants from you, and listen
to its answer . . . ask it why it wants that—what does
it really need? . . . And let it respond . . . ask it also
what it has to offer you, if you should meet its needs
. . . again allow the image to respond. . . .

Observe the image carefully again . . . is there anything about it you hadn't noticed before? . . . Does it look the same or is it different in any way? . . .

Now, in your imagination, allow yourself to *become* the image . . . what is it like to be the image? . . . Notice how you feel . . . notice what thoughts you have as the image . . . what would your life be like if you were this image? . . . Just sense what it's like to be this image. . . .

Through the eyes of the image, look back at yourself . . . what do you see? . . . Take a few minutes to really look at yourself from this new perspective . . . as the image, how do you feel about this person you are looking at . . . what do you think of this person? . . . What do you need from this person? . . . Speaking as the image, ask yourself for what you need. . . .

Now slowly become yourself again . . . the image has just told you what it needs from you . . . what, if anything, keeps you from meeting that need? . . . What issues or concerns seem to get in the way? . . . What might you do to change the situation and take a step toward meeting the image's needs? . . .

Allow an image to appear for your inner advisor, a wise, kind figure who knows you well . . . when you feel ready, ask your advisor about your symptom and its needs, and any thoughts, feelings, or circumstances that may make it hard for you to meet these needs . . . ask your advisor any questions you might have, and listen carefully to your advisor's responses . . . feel free to ask your advisor for help if you need it. . . .

Now, mentally review the conversation you have had with your symptom and your advisor from the beginning . . . if it feels right for you, choose one way that you can begin to meet your symptom's needs—some small but tangible way you can fill some part of its unmet needs . . . if you can't think of any way at all, ask your advisor for a suggestion. . . .

When you have thought of a way to begin meeting its needs, recall again the image that represents your symptom . . . ask it if it would be willing and able to give you tangible relief of symptoms if you take the steps you have thought of . . . if so, let the exchange begin . . . if not, ask it to tell you what you could do in exchange for perceptible relief . . . continue to dialogue until you have made a bargain or need to take a break from negotiating. . . .

Consider the image once more . . . is there anything you have learned from it or about it? . . . Is there anything that you appreciate about it? . . . If there is, take the time to express your appreciation to it . . . express anything else that seems important . . . and slowly come back to your waking state and take some time to write about your experience. . . .

Evaluating Your Experience

Take some time to write or draw anything significant to you in the experience. Describe your image of the symptom in detail. How does this image seem to relate to your experience of your symptoms or illness?

How did you feel about the image initially? Did your feelings change in any way as you continued to dialogue with this image? How do you feel about it now?

What did the image seem to want from you? What

did it say it needed? What did it say it had to offer you in return for meeting its needs?

How was it to become the image? Did you learn anything else about the image from this part of the imagery? As the image, what did you ask yourself for?

As yourself, what was your reaction to the image's request? Are there obstacles or barriers you became aware of to meeting its needs? If you chose to, how might you deal with them constructively? What would be a first step toward meeting your symptom's needs?

Did the image agree to give you tangible relief of symptoms if you took that step? Is there something else it wanted instead? Are you willing to make a bargain with it, or have you reached an impasse in negotiations? If so, you may want to take some time to think about what you could offer in exchange for relief. Consult with your advisor before returning to the dialogue with your symptoms.

You may not always be able to come to an agreement with your symptoms immediately. As with any negotiation, a good deal of exchange and consideration may need to take place before a bargain is struck. Make sure any agreement is mutually acceptable—one-sided pacts do not work. If you do make a bargain with your symptoms, keep your agreement and watch carefully for improvement.

The Next Steps

You may notice that as you write about this experience, you become aware of connections and information you didn't notice during the imagery. You may even notice yourself becoming aware of related information over several days following your inner dialogue. You may find information in dreams, in flashes of intuition, in books you are reading, from people you talk with, and TV shows you watch. Once you have asked the unconscious for advice, it responds in many ways. You may also find that repeating this process in a few days will allow you to penetrate even more deeply into the relationship between you and your symptom.

Once you've developed some insight into the meaning of your symptoms, an important question is often "What are you going to do about it?" Insight can stimulate change, but it may take continued awareness and action over time to make the change a part of your daily life. Psychoanalysis is often criticized for producing patients who understand everything they do, but do the same things they did when they entered therapy. It's not just the knowing, but the doing that counts. As Will Rogers once said, "You may be on the right track, but you'll get run over if you don't move."

While in some situations the imagery itself will have the effects you desire, in many others it will only point you in the direction you need to go. The process of grounding your insight, of using it to make tangible change in your life, is the key to converting the imaginary to the real. Paradoxically, imagery can help even in this down-to-earth step of self-healing. You will learn how in the next chapter.

TEN

Turning Insight Into Action

I have a favorite cartoon that features a little character who's saying, "My problem is, I can never separate my insight from my baloney!" That's what this chapter is about: separating insight from baloney. What difference does what you have learned so far make in your life? Does the insight you have gathered point you in a direction of change? Does it release you from negative feelings, thoughts, or attitudes? Will anything change in your life because of this information? *Could* anything change if you choose to act on your new knowledge, and if so, what needs to happen to bring about that change?

Bringing your insight down to earth can be called the process of *grounding*. In grounding, you take the imaginary and make it real. Without this step, your imagery work may remain mere fantasy.

Let's look at a simple example of grounding. Three men go to the doctor, complaining of shortness of breath. After examining them and conducting some tests, the doctor tells each of them they have early emphysema, a chronic disease of the lungs, and that they must stop smoking immediately or suffer progressive, disabling illness. If they stop smoking, it is likely that the disease will go no further. The first man crumples up his pack of cigarettes, throws it in the trash can, and never smokes again. The second man attempts to quit, finds it difficult, and backslides. He seeks help, and after several attempts, attending a number of stop-smoking programs and utilizing guided imagery, he quits. The third man makes a half-hearted attempt to cut down, but soon is smoking as before and continues to smoke in spite of deteriorating health.

What's the difference in these three men? We might expect it has something to do with their personalities, their life histories, and their ways of making change. It might have to do with the faith they have in their doctor's predictions. Ultimately, it has to do with *choice*. The first two men chose to quit smoking. For the first it was simple, for the second it took more work. The third never made the choice and by default chose to keep smoking.

The issue of choice is a critical one. We are always making choices that affect our health, from what we eat and breathe to whom we live with and what we do all day. Perhaps the ultimate choice is our view of life, whether to see it as a cup half-empty or half-full.

Choice has to do with will, and the act of grounding is an act of will. The *Oxford American Dictionary* defines will as "The mental faculty by which a person decides upon and controls his own actions or those of others."

Roberto Assagioli, the Italian psychiatrist who founded Psychosynthesis, describes the will as being similar to the helmsman of a boat. He is not the source of power for the boat, he is neither the engines nor the sails, but he mans the tiller and holds to the course to be sailed. In this metaphor, the imagination can be seen as a navigational tool. With it, we can take our bearings and look at possible courses that will take us to our chosen destination.

When we choose our course, that is an act of will, and each time we change or correct our course, that, too, is will. As the winds, tides, and currents of life interact with our plans, we need to hold fast to the tiller to maintain our course. There may be times when we need to change course to remain safe, yet we can still reach our destination by taking a different route. Sometimes we may need to change our direction and destination altogether.

In Assagioli's book, *The Act of Will,* he defines the "skillful will" as "the ability to obtain desired results with the least possible expenditure of energy." This skillfulness is different than simple "willpower," and imagination is one of its major components.

Assagioli describes six stages of willing. Dr. Naomi Remen has modified his model into a process which includes an extra imagery step, and her modification is the basis of the grounding method you will learn in this chapter. While I will describe the grounding process as a series of sequential steps, you may not always proceed from step to step. Sometimes several steps happen simultaneously, and at other times you may need to back up and repeat a step or two. If you are really stuck while trying to ground a particular insight, you may find going through the process step by step to be helpful.

The seven steps in this process are: 1) clarifying your aim, 2) deliberating on the possibilities, 3) choosing the one you will pursue, 4) affirming your choice, 5) planning your actions, 6) mentally rehearsing your plan, and 7) acting.

Let's look at our three smokers again. The first man, who quit on the spot, obviously spent little time in deliberation, but made a clear choice, and affirmed his choice with immediate action. He spent no time in planning or rehearsing, but acted directly and effectively. In effect, he turned his insight directly into action. The second man had the same goal, but needed more help. He deliberated a fair amount, both before and after attending and utilizing various forms of group and individual support. His choice, and affirmation, too, were apparently strong, since he stayed on course in spite of several setbacks. He spent a fair amount of time planning his stop-smoking strategies and used mental rehearsal and affirmation frequently. As he struggled with quitting, he maintained his awareness of the factors that helped him stay on course and those that tended to blow him off course. By continuing to pay attention, and affirming and reaffirming his choice, he reached his goal. The third man had the same information and the same resources available, but never really chose to quit. His real aim was not to be bothered and not to change. He didn't consider alternatives or supports, and never engaged the process in a conscious way. Of course, this is a choice, too, and the strength of his will can be seen in his continuation of smoking in the face of a crippling, and ultimately fatal disease.

Assagioli points out that the "stages of will are like the links in a chain; therefore, the chain itself—that is, the act of willing—is only as strong as its weakest link." He also says, "It has been my observation . . . that the principal cause of failure in completing an act of will is that people often have difficulty carrying out one or another specific stage . . . they get stuck at a particular point in the sequence. Therefore, understanding the various stages and their functions is most valuable in uncovering the specific weak point, or points, in which one needs to become more proficient."

The Stages of Willing

Let's take a closer look at each stage. Perhaps you will recognize the stages which are easy for you and the ones that need more attention.

The first step in the act of grounding is to *clarify* your goal, to become as clear as possible about what it is you wish to do. One way to do that is to write down the simplest, clearest statement of your goal. Take the time to go over your written sentence carefully, and make sure each word is necessary and appropriate. Dr. Remen suggests that you then circle the most important word in the sentence. This can be quite illuminating.

Al, a forty-year-old insurance salesman suffering from recurring back-pain, realized from his work with his inner advisor that he needed to learn to be more relaxed. He wrote the following sentence: "I will learn to be more relaxed."

Notice how the sense of Al's declaration changes depending on the word he identifies as the most important. If he circles "I" or "will," it emphasizes the place of choice, responsibility, and determination in accomplishing this goal, while if "learn" is more important, it points to the process of acquiring information and skills as the central element. "Relaxed" may indicate that even in this endeavor the key thing to remember is to take it easy, while "more" might tell him he's got the tools but has to put them to work more consistently. "Be" as the most important word may lead to a change in perspective from "doing" to "being" that leads to a more relaxed way of living. Play with your own sentence and notice what seems to be the most important element in it.

Once you've become clear on what it is you want to do, you enter the stage of *deliberation*. This is a brainstorming step where you generate possibilities. The brainstorming technique consists of writing down any and all ways you can think of to accomplish your purpose, without stopping to edit or evaluate the feasibility of the idea. Write quickly and record anything that comes to mind, no matter how silly, unrealistic, far-fetched, or unappealing. Brainstorming frees your mind to express all its ideas and to generate new ones. It's a creative process similar to the process of evolution in nature. Nature generates all kinds of variations in life forms. The ones that "work" best live longest and reproduce, the ones that don't work don't survive. Let this same creative process work for you in brainstorming—don't edit, just write.

Al wrote down the following possibilities for learning to be more relaxed: drinking less coffee, learning a deep relaxation technique, getting massages, drinking more alcohol, leaving his job and going to Tahiti, playing cards with his friends, watching more TV, watching less TV, spending a day a week with his kids, taking up a new hobby, robbing a bank (he was under financial pressure), asking for a raise, changing jobs, going back to school so he could get a better job, and becoming a monk.

Brainstorming is a process which may engage the creative abilities of your silent, imaginative mind. It is also a step where imagery could be helpful in expanding your list of options. One of the best ways to engage the creative potential of your image-making mind is to ask your inner advisor for suggestions. Al's inner advisor confirmed that giving up coffee and regular relaxation exercises would be the best place to start. His advisor also reminded him that he had always been able to get by financially, and that he would be able to do whatever was necessary to get through the particularly hard time he was currently having. This was reassuring to Al, and he was perceptibly more relaxed after this inner dialogue.

The third step in grounding is to *choose* the best option for you. As you look over your list of possibilities, some will obviously be more feasible or attractive to you. Some you will eliminate as nonsensical. Several possibilities may combine into one. Perhaps a few more will occur to you. Choose the best one for you, the one you are most likely to carry out successfully. It often helps to look for the *easiest* option as a first choice as long as it is one that is likely to create some definite movement in your chosen direction. Choosing the "right-sized step" is a crucial aspect of grounding; a step that is big enough to make a difference but not so big that it becomes overwhelming. Let's say you have diabetes and need to lose sixty pounds of excess weight. The idea of six months of strict dieting may be so anxiety-producing that you run to the refrigerator for some comfort. If you break your goal down, however, into steps that are shorter-term and more tangible, it becomes easier to work toward. In other words, what if you decide to lose four pounds in the next two weeks? And, when that has been accomplished, another four pounds the two weeks after that? By taking one step at a time, you can eventually reach your longer-term target with a minimum of anxiety and struggle.

When you choose your option, circle it, or write it down again. Al chose to learn a deep relaxation technique and use it at least once a day. He also decided to drink only one cup of coffee in the morning and one in the afternoon, as opposed to his previous habit of six to eight cups a day.

Affirmation is the next step. Put your energy behind your choice. It may be helpful to say what you will do out loud, even if you are alone, and repeat it a few times. You can frequently get a sense of how much energy you can really commit to this choice by the sound of your voice. If it sounds too tentative, you might want to reconsider and choose a step that you can take with more confidence. You can also stick with a choice in spite of feeling tentative, realizing that it will take a little more commitment than you initially realized.

The next stage is *planning*. Make a detailed plan that describes exactly how you will go about accomplishing your goal. What needs to happen? Who do you need to talk to, and what do you have to do? What's the first step, and what comes next? In a real sense, all planning involves imagery, and this step and the next, mental rehearsal, often blend or overlap.

Mental rehearsal consists of relaxing and imagining yourself carrying out the plan you have created. Take it slow, imagine it as if it were happening as you do it, and include as much detail as possible. Mental rehearsal can both affirm and troubleshoot your plan. You will often be able to anticipate obstacles and adjust for them in your planning.

Our man Al, for instance, planned to cut down on coffee as part of his effort to learn to relax. He imagined himself going to his usual breakfast spot on the way to work. He imagined himself sitting down and saying hello to his favorite waitress, who immediately brought him a cup of coffee. He noticed in his imagery that as he read the paper, she automatically refilled his cup whenever it was empty. He realized he better ask her not to do that and later made a note of it as part of his revised plan. Another part of his plan included practicing a relaxation technique for half an hour each evening before dinner. As he imagined himself arriving home, he saw he would need to talk with his wife and his son and ask for their support during that time. He noticed that even imagining asking for that time to himself made him feel a little nervous. As he tuned deeper into that feeling, he found he felt somewhat guilty about taking time to "loaf" at home. He discussed his concerns with his inner advisor, who said that putting energy into staying well was not loafing and would pay off for everyone in the family, since he would be more pleasant to be with after relaxing. His advisor also suggested that he could make a point of spending some special time with his wife and son after dinner.

The following script will guide you, step by step, through the grounding process I have described. It is different from the scripts you have used up to now in that it does not require you to enter a deeply relaxed state until you reach the stage of mental rehearsal. Have writing materials at hand, and take as much time as you need to work through each stage, either reading one section at a time, or turning the tape player on and off as needed. There is no predetermined time period for this process. It could take you as little as thirty minutes and as much as the rest of your life, depending on the magnitude of the issue you are working with, the clarity of your insight, and the presence or absence of resistance to your change.

SCRIPT:

Turning Insight Into Action

Take a comfortable position, and have writing materials at hand . . . during this exercise you will often have your eyes open and will be writing . . . there is no need to do deep relaxation until you reach the stage of mental rehearsal. . . .

The process of grounding is something you may or may not do well instinctively . . . the following process breaks it down into steps that allow you to make change happen from your insights. . . .

The first step is to *clarify your insight* . . . take some time to state to yourself as clearly and simply as you can what you have learned that you wish to act on. . . . Write down the clearest sentence you can that expresses that insight . . . carefully look at the sentence you have written and decide which word is the most important one in that sentence . . . look at each word carefully and make sure that it is just the right word to express exactly what you mean . . . take as much time as you need to do this. . . .

Next, *think about your insight* and list several possible ways you might practically act on that insight to make the changes you desire . . .brainstorm this—take a large sheet of paper and write down as many ways as you can think of that would be a step in this direction . . . do not edit as you write . . . list all possibilities that come to mind, whether realistic or not. . . .

Look over your options—can you combine any? . . . Which would be the most practical for you to actually carry out? . . . Which would be the simplest? . . . The easiest? . . . Is there one way which promises the most success or the greatest return for the least effort? . . .

When you are ready, *choose* the option that seems the most realistic and promising for you . . . circle that choice on your list. . . .

The next step is to *affirm* your choice . . . to put your energy and resolve behind it . . . it often helps to state your choice aloud . . . repeat to yourself several times "I choose to . . ." whatever it is you have decided to do . . . make your affirmation out loud. . . .

The fifth step is to *make a concrete plan* for carrying out your choice . . . consider what specific steps are involved and in what order . . . who might you have to speak to, and what might you have to do? . . . Make a specific plan in simple, yet detailed steps . . . write it down, making sure it is clear and practical. . . .

Now *rehearse your plan in your imagination* . . . close your eyes and take a couple of deep breaths . . . invite your body to relax as it has so many times before . . .

just allow it to be at ease and comfortable where you
are . . . as you breathe gently and easily, allow your
mind to become quiet and still . . . you may want to
go to your quiet inner place and become comfortable
there . . . when you are ready, imagine yourself actually carrying out your plan . . . really use your imagination to see and feel yourself carrying out your plan
from start to finish to give yourself a sense of what
may happen in real life . . . notice which parts seem
easy and which parts are harder . . . during your imagery you may become aware of obstacles to carrying
out your plan . . . these may be events, people, or
simply feelings and attitudes which arise as you begin
to act on your plan . . . if you do envision such obstacles, adjust your plan to account for them . . . you may
find you need to change your plan or break it down
into smaller steps to make it happen . . . take all the
time you need to adjust your plan until you can imagine yourself carrying it out successfully . . . repeat your
imagery rehearsal, imagining yourself successfully
carrying out your plan several times, until you feel
comfortable with it . . . this will help you energize
and support this new way of acting and reacting for
you. . . .

When you are ready, open your eyes and come
wide-awake . . . take some time to write about any
changes or adjustments you've made in your plan . . .
and about any obstacles you have anticipated and how
you might deal with them if they arise. . . .

The final step in grounding is to *act* on your plan.
Carry it out in real life for a certain amount of time
. . . as you do this, continue to be observant of your
thoughts and feelings . . . notice how others react to

you as you act in this new way . . . notice where you
are successful and where you enjoy this new way . . .
and also notice where you have difficulty, if you do.
. . . Do any problems you didn't anticipate arise as you
act on this plan? . . . If so, how might you adjust to
account for them? . . . Life is a continuous process of
adjustment and refinement . . . pay attention, and you
can learn to make change happen in the easiest and
most effective way. . . .

Longer-Term Grounding

At first, you may want to ground insights for a few
hours, a day, or a week at a time. As you learn the
process, you will find it easier to ground insights over
longer and longer periods.

Your journal will help you see the changes you
have made over time and the ways you have made
them. Reviewing your journal periodically may reveal
patterns that you have worked through before so you
can learn to anticipate, change, or avoid repeating them.

Two other techniques I learned in Psychosynthesis
training are useful in helping you sustain a new attitude
or behavior over longer periods. They are the "Morning Preview" and the "Evening Review."

In the "Morning Preview" you take time at the
beginning of the day to visualize or mentally rehearse
your chosen plan of action, imagining yourself interacting with the people and events you expect to encounter
that day. Rehearsing in this way energizes and rein-
forces your plan, gives you a chance to tailor it to the

specific situations you anticipate, and makes it easier to carry out.

To do an "Evening Review," take some time at the end of the day. Close your eyes, relax, and run the day through in your mind, beginning in the morning, then the afternoon, and the evening. Notice what went well and what not as well. How could things be done better tomorrow, or the next time you'll need to act in this way? As you review, avoid becoming critical or judgmental about yourself. This is an opportunity to learn and refine your plan from the feedback life gives you.

The more you use imagery and grounding techniques, the easier they will become to use. Yet there may be times when you find it difficult to use any techniques, even ones that have worked well for you in the past. This may alert you to the presence of resistance. Resistance, like a symptom, is not a bad thing. It just lets you know there's something you need to know more about before you can move on. The next chapter will teach you to use imagery techniques you already know to deal respectfully and effectively with resistance.

ELEVEN

Resistance—The Loyal Opposition

At some time during the process of change you may encounter resistance. The surest sign of resistance is finding yourself cleaning up a two-year-old mess in the basement instead of doing your inner work. You may feel that *anything* seems easier than taking another step on the path of self-knowledge and healing.

The term "resistance" in psychotherapy refers to the curious but common phenomenon of a person who seeks change acting as if he or she doesn't want to change at all. Resistance occurs when you run into your psychological defenses, the barriers we all have to becoming conscious of thoughts or feelings that threaten to be too difficult to bear.

People who are not well trained in psychology may feel it's bad or wrong to be resistant. Even professional counselors and therapists sometimes react to resistance this way, and become frustrated and angry at "resistant clients." This is unfortunate and represents a fundamental misunderstanding of the nature of resistance.

Psychological defenses are a necessary component

of healthy psychological functioning. Each of us has experienced grief, sadness, anger, and fear. If we were to remain conscious of it all, we would very likely be unable to function in our day-to-day lives. Defenses maintain a barrier between our conscious awareness and our unconscious processes and memories. This allows us to shut out the past and future and pay attention to the present. In psychosis, psychological defenses fail, and people are overwhelmed by a flood of normally unconscious material. Coping with this overflow of inner perception leaves them unable to take care of themselves in their outer lives.

While inner mechanisms of defense may be normal and healthy, they may sometimes become a barrier to desirable changes you are trying to make. This may be because the defenses have become ineffective, outdated, or distorted; or because they represent valid concerns that require consideration as you change.

What Does Resistance Look Like?

In a therapeutic relationship, resistance may show itself in many ways. Missed appointments, habitual lateness for appointments, unpaid bills, and endless talking about superficial details of life may all be signs of resistance. While there may be other reasons for any of these circumstances, most therapists will point them out to clients and ask if they are aware of any feelings of reluctance to going deeper in the therapy. This is often a crucially important juncture in therapy, and deserves careful consideration when you are working on your own.

Resistance as you work alone could manifest in many different ways:

—not doing relaxation/imagery as planned
—letting other things get in the way
—doing relaxation but no imagery, especially if you have used imagery before
—using imagery but not in relation to your issue/concern/symptom
—your imagery fades away
—your imagery becomes hard to understand
—developing insight into your problem but not acting on it
—feeling discomfort or anxiety while doing imagery
—feeling discomfort or anxiety as you begin to ground your insights
—unusual difficulty or frustration with any stage of the process

Please don't be self-critical if you think you are manifesting resistance. Your task is not to judge yourself, but to make an honest assessment of what is going on before deciding what to do about it.

How Do I Deal With Resistance?

The approach I favor in dealing with resistance is very similar to the approach we took in dealing with symptoms. If you encounter resistance, take the time to explore it respectfully, and find out why it's there.

Include it in your process of healing, and you may find an ally in what first seemed to be a foe.

When you are remodeling a house, sometimes you want to knock down walls to reshape the space or to make more room. Before you do that, however, you want to be sure the wall you are taking out isn't supporting the ceiling. If it is, you will either have to find a way to include it in your design or find another way to support the ceiling before you begin. Otherwise the roof may come down on your head. It's the same with "remodeling" your mind—take the time to find out what things are doing there before you decide to blast them away.

How do you find out what purpose your resistance may have? You've probably guessed what I'm going to say. You ask it! As in "Listening to Your Symptom," you let an image form for it and have a conversation with it. Find out what it is, what it does for you, how it got there, how it feels about the changes you want to make, and whether there's a way to meet its needs yet allow the change to happen. You can use the script at the end of this chapter to do that when you're ready, but first, let me share a couple of case histories with you that show how useful it can be to work with your resistance.

Max was a man in his fifties who had been diagnosed as having a recurrence of cancer. His oncologist offered him a course of rigorous chemotherapy with the apology that "Unfortunately, for this kind of tumor, the response rate is very low." Nevertheless, Max had begun the treatments in the hopes that it would help. He also came to me to learn to work with imagery for the same reason.

Max was a very bright, well-educated man who had studied the medical literature regarding his alternatives and likely prognosis. He was afraid he had very little chance to survive this recurrence. He expressed his doubts many times about being able to use imagery because he was such a "concrete thinker." We started by having him draw a picture of his tumor, his immune system, and his treatment.

The initial pictures were very inert. The tumor was a black blob behind a wall. There were few immune cells, and they were just hanging around the outside of the wall. Initially Max didn't even draw the chemotherapy. Over a number of sessions I encouraged him to take a closer look at the image of the tumor and the wall. Each step was excruciatingly slow. The blob was inert. The wall was inert. There was very little sense of movement or energy in his imagery or his drawings.

While from week to week there were minor changes in his imagery, there was a sense of holding back in Max's approach to this work. Weeks later he had progressed to imagining white cells in the form of leeches flowing in and attaching themselves to the tumor. The trouble was, they just seemed to be sitting on it. He wasn't able to imagine the tumor shrinking or any real aggressiveness or activity on the part of his "leeches." So there was movement, but it was agonizingly slow, especially for a person challenged by an aggressive, fast-moving tumor.

It finally dawned on me that perhaps there was something standing in the way of Max being more active in his imagery, and I mentioned this possibility to him. He agreed to do a session to explore unconscious sources of resistance.

I asked him to allow an image to appear of any part of him that objected to his getting better, and a large rock came to his mind. It was gray and, unsurprisingly, quite inert. It was hard to get anything out of it. I encouraged him to explore the rock, and he found himself around its back side, where it seemed to be a hill he could walk up. He found himself on top of the rock, which he now described as a high bluff overlooking a deep, dark chasm. I asked him if he had any sense of where he needed to go from here, since neither the rock nor hill would "talk" with him, and he saw an identical bluff across the chasm. On top of this other bluff were his wife and two children, all waving for him to come over. As he saw this, Max showed the first sign of any emotion I'd seen in him since our work began.

I asked him if he wanted to go across the chasm. He said he would like to but there was no way to do it.

"How do you imagine you could cross that chasm?" I asked.

"I'd have to throw a rope over to them, then another, and they could tie it down. Then I could lay planks across it and build a bridge."

I suggested that in his imagination he could have a rope if he needed one and a rope appeared to him. Then he began to despair. "I'm not strong enough—I can't throw it all the way across."

"What do you need in order to be able to throw it all the way across?"

"Strength," he said. "I need more strength."

We then spent the rest of the session having him recall times in his life when he was strong—physically, mentally, and emotionally. Each time he recalled an incident where he was strong, he was encouraged to pay very close attention to how it felt to be strong, and to feel this strength inside him. He enjoyed this greatly and commented on its similarity to building physical strength through exercise. He practiced this for a week, and the next week we returned to the bluff in his imagination.

Now he was able to imagine throwing the rope over the chasm that separated him from his family. He saw them enthusiastically catching the rope and tying it down. He threw another and began building his bridge, completing it within the session and crossing over it to be lovingly welcomed.

Following this, we talked about what the imagery might mean in the context of his real life. He began to express his feelings about some difficulties in the family, about trying to protect the family from his own fears, and the feelings of isolation that caused in him. As we talked, he became aware of how important it was to him to resolve some old family conflicts and to be able to be himself in his struggle to get well. He initiated some family talks, and they saw a family counselor for a while. Max found the process extremely helpful and emotionally liberating. As the family communication improved, Max became more relaxed, felt happier than he had in a long time, and his healing imagery became much more active and aggressive.

Jason was a twenty-four-year-old actor with asthma since childhood. He was quite adept at imagery and found that deep relaxation and simple visualization of opening his bronchial tubes widely could help him breathe more easily with less medication. He was pleased to find he had this ability and used it successfully for almost a year.

Then he stopped doing it regularly, and his asthma grew gradually worse until he came in one day wheezing audibly.

He said that he had met a woman he was spending a lot of time with and didn't have the time to do imagery. I asked him to relax and ask if there was any part of him that was standing in the way of his using his mind to help himself feel better. An image of a small, somewhat agitated dwarf dressed like a Roman soldier came into his mind. The dwarf's name was Romeo. He said he was "on guard" and the "roads in were closed until further orders." He said he was "protecting the kingdom within" and had had his job ever since he could remember. Jason felt strongly that the roads were symbolic both of his bronchial tubes and the "road to my heart." On further exploration with the dwarf Romeo, Jason began to see how his asthma, while sometimes bringing him sympathy as a child, really served to cut him off from intimate relationships in his life. He recalled several flare-ups associated with budding romances, and the embarrassment it had brought him, yet he also felt that at some level it was trying to protect him from heartache.

The direction of Jason's work now started to focus on how Romeo could protect him from emotional pain while allowing interchange along the "roads" that led inside. Jason imagined an elaborate series of checkpoints at various distances from the center of his "kingdom," which showed itself as an image of a heart. He experimented with allowing images of different people to reach different checkpoints, and noticed how that felt. He issued imaginary "passes" and "security clearances" for people, and found that rather than being unconsciously "closed up tight," he was able to become more intimate with some people. He started to use his remaining asthmatic reactions as signs of the need to pay attention to his feelings, and over time found them a valuable guide to developing healthier relationships.

Jason found his "resistance" to be a loyal ally, trying to do a necessary job with inadequate training and support. As he realized the important function of his resistance he was able to help it carry out its function more effectively, and found it to be an important part of his movement toward greater wholeness.

Laziness: Another Form of Resistance

I've said that resistance is often a manifestation of a psychological defense that needs exploration. There is, however, a common source of resistance that may not represent more deeply seated issues. Laziness. While laziness may be due to underlying defenses, it may have simply become a way of life and may need to be overcome with some will and commitment.

The American dream of easy, simple solutions for complex problems can work against you if you let it. Imagery and self-exploration are not always easy. They can require effort and discipline. Paying attention to your thoughts, feelings, and ideas takes patience, skill, courage, and mental energy. Even though you may be learning about yourself in a very exciting way, it takes some doing to take the time, learn the skills, decipher the lessons, and put them into action.

To overcome resistance born of laziness, you need motivation. Remind yourself of the reasons you decided to learn about imagery in the first place. Keep your vision of the best health you can imagine in front of you. Talk with other people who are enthusiastic about imagery—if possible, talk with people who have used it to help themselves. Reread any parts of this book that have intrigued, interested, or perhaps inspired you. Read other inspirational books or articles you have found about imagery. Use tapes to guide you—they make imagery easier to do, and can support you in your learning process. Seek out groups or professionals who use imagery if you need more support to get going.

Simple resistance due to inertia will usually respond rather quickly to pushing ahead and practicing for a week. Mild resistance will disappear, and before you know it, you'll be moving along and making progress. If the resistance is more profound and important, it will persist or reappear. If something repeatedly seems to get in your way, stop and pay attention to it.

Treat this type of resistance as you would treat a symptom. Acknowledge its presence, assume it is there for a reason, and the reason is not necessarily bad.

The imagery process that follows offers you the opportunity to have an inner dialogue with an image of your resistance. Find out what it is, what it's doing there, what it wants, what it needs, and what it's trying to do for you. You may be surprised to find it a helpful force rather than an obstruction, one that can help you avoid possible problems. Whether you find it helpful or not, it is an aspect of yourself that needs to be dealt with, and it deserves to be dealt with respectfully.

Through imagery you can learn more about any inner concern or objection to proceeding on your current path. Use the following script in the same way you have used the previous guided imagery scripts. Take approximately thirty to forty-five minutes to complete this exploration. Be open, gentle, and nonjudgmental with yourself and any images that come.

SCRIPT:

Learning From Your Resistance

Take a comfortable position and loosen any tight clothing or restrictive jewelry . . . make sure you will not be disturbed for thirty minutes or so. . . .

Begin to relax by taking a couple of deep, full breaths, letting the exhalations be real "letting go" breaths . . . invite your body and mind to begin to release and relax any tension you may be holding with each out breath . . . allow the relaxation to happen naturally . . . easily . . . as it has so many times before . . . no need to be concerned about how quickly or how deeply relaxed you go . . . merely allowing the pleasant, comfortable sensations of relaxation to deepen in your body as your mind becomes quiet, still, and at ease. . . .

When you are ready, imagine yourself going to your special, peaceful inner place . . . a place of great beauty, peacefulness, and security for you . . . this may be a place you've visited before, either in your imagination or in outer life, or it may be a place that occurs to you right now . . . it doesn't really matter where you imagine yourself to be as long as it is a place of peacefulness, quiet, safety, and communion for you

. . . take some time to look around you and notice
what you see in this place . . . notice what you hear
. . . and what you smell . . . and especially how good it
feels to be in this place, a special place of rest, of comfort, of healing for you. . . .

Find the spot in this special place where you feel
most centered, most calm, most aware, and become
comfortable in that spot . . . sense the connection, the
centeredness, the quiet calm you feel in this spot . . .
from here, you can observe and notice and learn. . . .

When you are ready, ask within yourself if any
part of you has any objection to or concern about your
continuing on the path of healing you have begun . . .
just ask, quietly listen, and wait for an answer . . . let
all your inner parts know that this is a place of healing,
and that all parts are welcome to state their concerns
and opinions on matters that concern them . . . let all
your parts know that you are sincerely interested to
know of any objections to the course you have begun,
and that all concerns will get a fair hearing. . . .

If all is quiet, and you sense there is no objection,
you may want to spend some time imagining yourself
taking the next step in your healing process, or you
may want to invite your inner advisor to appear and
have a talk . . . if there is an objection, invite any part
of you that has an objection to appear in your quiet
place so you can understand its concerns. . . .

Observe the image that forms to represent this
part or parts . . . if there is more than one, notice
which seems to attract your attention the most, or
which seems strongest . . . if there are many parts, ask
them to appoint a spokesman who can represent their
needs . . . as you observe that image, notice what it

looks like and what qualities it conveys to you . . .
notice any feelings that come up in you as you observe
this image. . . .

Thank the image for coming into your awareness,
and invite it to be comfortable there with you . . .
when it feels right, ask the image about its concerns or
objections . . . allow the image to communicate with
you in a way you can understand . . . accept for now
what it communicates, whether you agree with it or
not, whether it makes sense to you or not . . . ask any
questions you may have so you can be as clear as
possible on the nature of its concerns. . . .

Consider what the image has communicated to
you . . . do you understand its objection, concern, or
fear? . . . Can you see any validity in its objection? . . .
If its objection were dealt with effectively, if its needs
were truly met, would it be willing to stop its opposition to your movement? Ask it and let it answer . . .
Ask it if it can imagine any way that you can move in
the direction you've chosen and meet its needs at the
same time. . . .

Invite your inner advisor to be there with you,
and welcome it into your awareness . . . let your
advisor know about this part's concerns, and ask your
advisor if it can suggest some ways that the part's
needs can be met, while continuing in the direction
of healing . . . listen carefully to your advisor's
responses. . . .

Consider each suggestion and possibility . . . if
any of them seem feasible, imagine carrying them out,
and notice how the concerns of the objecting part can
be met while the movement toward healing continues
. . . there may even be ways that the part can now

contribute to your healing . . . imagine this happening successfully. . . .

If no ideas come to mind for how this can be done, ask both the concerned part and your advisor if they would be willing to work on this problem for a few days, searching the unconscious for new, creative, yet practical ways to include all your parts in this healing . . . arrange a time to meet again in three or four days to discuss the possibilities. . . .

When this is finished, ask if there are any other concerns or objections within . . . if there are, repeat the process to account for these concerns. . . .

If there are a great many concerns, this may be something you will need to work on through several sessions . . . let all concerned parts know that you value their input and will do your best to find a fair way of including them all in your healing process . . . let them know that they are all parts of one greater whole, and that your desire is for each of them to be happier, healthier parts of that wholeness . . . invite their participation and ask them all to find ways to work together in greater harmony. . . .

When you are finished for today, thank all your inner parts . . . the ones that came today to participate and the ones working out of your consciousness . . . and affirm your desire for a healthier working relationship among them all . . . imagine in some way all parts of you together . . . parts you know and parts you don't yet know . . . parts you like and those you don't . . . parts you understand and parts you need to understand better . . . all together as part of one larger whole, connected and working together in harmony. . . .

And when you are ready, open your eyes, come wide-awake and alert, and take some time to write about what you have learned. . . .

Evaluating Your Experience

What images formed as you asked for any parts with concerns to appear? Were there more than one? What was the main image like? What were its concerns or objections to your continuing your work at this time?

How do you feel about its concerns? Do they seem valid to you? Were you willing to look for ways to attend to its concerns while continuing your healing work?

Were you able to imagine a way in which this can happen? Does it seem feasible to you? Are you willing to put it into action?

Do you sense other concerns or objections that need attention? If so, you will want to work with this process again until they have been cleared.

Were you able to imagine all your parts working together as part of a larger whole? What was that like? Were any parts left out? If so, see if you can bring them into the fold next time you imagine this.

Consider again what you have learned about your resistance. Perhaps you can put yourself in the place of the part that objected and understand its concerns. Perhaps you have seen some ways to meet its needs and continue in your work. If not, you can be aware over the next few days of any ideas that come to you in your imagery sessions, your dreams, or your daily life. As you repeat this exercise, you will learn more about moving forward as a whole, while considering the needs of your various parts.

You will find that parts are like people, and your parts are most like you—they are you. Some parts will just be timid, and they need reassurance from you or from a stronger part. Others are trying to protect you and fear that the changes you are considering may bring you harm. Their fear needs to be addressed and their desire to protect you validated. It's not that they shouldn't protect you but that you need to help them find a way to protect you, yet allow you to grow and change. It may be possible to do both if you help the part move beyond its habitual way of doing things.

All your parts are there for a reason. When they make their presence known through resistance, invite them for a talk, find out what they need and how they function in you, and what they can contribute to you as a whole person. Help them do their jobs well, and they may turn out to be your most loyal and effective allies in healing.

TWELVE

Checking Your Progress

By now you have learned to relax, imagined better health, discussed your situation with an inner advisor, listened to your symptom, turned your insights into action, and come to terms with any remaining resistance.

How are you feeling? What have you learned? Has your health changed since you began to work this way? Has your way of thinking about health changed?

It might be worthwhile at this point to assess your progress. It's easy to take improvement for granted as you focus on current symptoms or problems. Reviewing your journal and your process from the beginning will help you notice any progress you have made.

Give yourself credit for your work even if you are still having problems with your health. Healing is not an all-or-nothing phenomenon, especially if you have a chronic illness. Acknowledge your progress even as you recognize the need to continue working toward better health. Don't overlook or disparage improvement because you were hoping for a cure.

If you are improved, keep working—you are going in the right direction. What do you think has made the most difference for you? What are the most important lessons you have learned or changes you have made? What still remains to be done? Continue to relax, and imagine healing on a regular basis. Stay in touch with your inner advisor, and continue your inner dialogue with any symptoms that remain.

If you haven't improved, carefully review the ways you have been using the techniques you have learned. Consider the following questions in your assessment:

1) Are you really able to relax? When you practice relaxation and imagine yourself in a quiet place, do you feel a physical relaxation and become relatively quiet mentally? If not, find a way to do this successfully. A good deal of the effectiveness of the imagery depends on your ability to develop a quiet state of inner concentration.

If you are reading the scripts, or using your own tapes, try using professionally recorded relaxation tapes. If you have been using prerecorded tapes, try some others. One may work better for you than the others, and listening to several may help you find your own way to relax. A number of good tapes are listed in the Resource Guide. They are inexpensive, and often make it easier to learn to relax.

If tapes don't help, look for stress reduction, relaxation, self-hypnosis, yoga, or meditation workshops in your area that provide instruction in relaxation. If you still have trouble, seek out a qualified biofeedback therapist who will help you learn to achieve deep physiologic relaxation.

2) Are you using relaxation and healing imagery techniques frequently enough? If you haven't been doing a minimum of two sessions a day, for fifteen to twenty minutes at a time, consider a two-week trial of *regular* practice at that frequency, then reevaluate.

3) Are you able to visualize, feel, or otherwise sense a process of healing happening within you as you do your healing imagery? Can you even pretend it is happening? Experiment with your imagery until you can imagine this happening in a way that is believable to you.

4) Do you believe that healing is possible for you? Are you enthusiastic about the possibility or are you just going through the motions? If so, why? You don't need to believe healing *will* happen, but you do need to believe it *could* happen.

5) Do you need to know more about imagery to be able to believe it can help? If so, use the Resource Guide to find books, tapes, centers, and people who can provide you with the information or guidance you need.

6) Have you made any agreements, promises, or bargains with inner figures that you haven't kept? Review your journal and imagery experiences to be sure. If you have ignored or forgotten about an agreement you made, relax, go to your quiet place, and reconnect with the image concerned. Explain why you didn't keep the bargain, and apologize if it seems appropriate. Be honest in your dialogue. After all, there's no one to fool but yourself. Ask the image for another chance, and if you make any new promises, be certain to keep them.

Treat this process with respect if you hope to use it successfully.

7) Is there some other part of you that needs to be heard? Use the resistance script to invite any such part into your awareness. Continue to repeat this process as often as necessary if symptoms continue or recur.

 If you have done all the above, and feel that you have worked as hard as you can but still feel no better, stop trying for a while. You may be working too hard. One of the principles in healing through imagery is the use of "passive will." While you imagine the outcome you desire, you maintain a relaxed, almost detached state of mind. Trying too hard can actually block the effects of your imagery. David Bresler says it's like trying to come up with a urine sample at the doctor's office. Giving up for a while may allow the healing you have been imagining to begin.
 If you continue to have trouble, you may want to consult with a qualified health professional who works with guided imagery.
 Whatever you do, be gentle with yourself and avoid self-criticism and blame. No one knows the limits and potentials of this type of healing. While some people at some times under some circumstances are capable of miraculous recoveries from dire illness, others who have worked conscientiously do not physically heal. Ultimately, everyone suffers from one illness or incident from which they don't recover. Even then, imagery can lead to important healing at emotional and spiritual levels.
 There are no guarantees in healing, just as there are

no guarantees in life. If your work with imagery has not produced the healing you hoped for, at least you have tried. You have done your part. If you have given it your best effort, no one can expect more.

Whatever your experience with imagery and healing, please consider sharing it with me. If you have had an unexpected or remarkable recovery, or if you have had a problem working with this method, write me in care of the publisher. Your letters will be forwarded to me personally and will be handled with the strictest professional confidentiality. Your experience may help all of us develop a deeper understanding of this process.

THIRTEEN

Imagery, Prevention, and Wellness

Imagery is not only a set of tools for healing, but for preventing illness and living the highest quality daily life. It can help you create a life of meaning, of purpose, and of wellness. Wellness is the positive aspect of the health spectrum, extending the yardstick of health far beyond the absence of disease. John Travis, M.D., a California physician and co-author of *The Wellness Workbook,* first brought this concept into focus in the late 1960s. Dr. Travis's model of health extends from illness on one side of the scale to the rich, expansive awareness and enjoyment of life he calls wellness on the other. The diagram below illustrates the scope of this model.

Healing can be considered to be the movement from the left side of the scale toward the right, and it happens all along the continuum. The imagery skills you have learned can assist your movement toward wellness whether you are ill or currently healthy but desire an even fuller, more satisfying life. Imagery can help you solve practical problems, develop insight into others, improve your relationships, enhance your self-confidence, and help you reach the goals you set for yourself.

How can imagery assist this movement toward greater wellness? To begin with, regular relaxation can reduce stress, restore your vitality, and perhaps reduce your vulnerability to illness. It will almost certainly improve the quality of your day. The many benefits of relaxation as a practice are detailed in Chapter Three.

As you relax, you may want to spend some time imagining a healthy, vital flow of blood and energy circulating throughout your body, reaching every tissue and cell and bathing you in radiant, healing light. Or you might want to imagine yourself healthy, happy, and doing the things you love to do, and being with the people you love to be with. You may develop an image of radiant health that is personally meaningful, and imagine it being within you always.

If you have a special goal, such as better relationships, improved athletic or work performance, or enhanced creativity, you may want to imagine yourself being successful in achieving that goal. Make the image as vivid and clear as possible, and imagine it happening in the present. Use the image as an affirmation, and notice what happens in that area of your life.

Who couldn't use a chat with a wise, loving guide from time to time? Use your inner advisor as a way to connect with your own wisdom and creativity. Your advisor may be helpful to you in solving problems, resolving conflicts, and staying aligned with your feelings, values, purpose, and sense of well-being.

The inner dialogue techniques you learned in the chapters on listening to your symptoms and working with resistance can be used to help you gain insight into

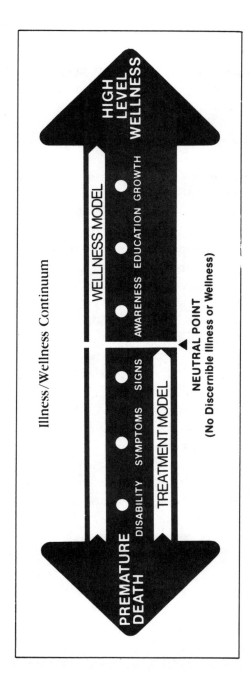

Illness/Wellness Continuum

Illness/Wellness Continuum

WELLNESS MODEL

HIGH LEVEL WELLNESS

AWARENESS   EDUCATION   GROWTH

TREATMENT MODEL

DISABILITY   SYMPTOMS   SIGNS

PREMATURE DEATH

▲ NEUTRAL POINT
(No Discernible Illness or Wellness)

ILLNESS/WELLNESS CONTINUUM used with permission, Copyright 1972, 1981, John Travis, M.D., Wellness Associates, Box 5433, Mill Valley, CA 94942. From *Wellness Workbook*, Ryan & Travis, Ten Speed Press, 1981, 1987.

almost any problem or issue you want to understand
more fully. Using this technique with minor signs and
symptoms may allow you to respond to them effectively before they go on to become more difficult problems. Working with parts can help you avoid or resolve
inner conflicts, harmonize and unify the "community
within," and mobilize resources and energy you may
not know you had.

The grounding process and imagery rehearsal can
help you move more effectively toward any goal you
choose, from stopping smoking, drinking, or overeat-
ing to making your plans and dreams into reality.

Wherever you begin on the scale of health, imagery
can help you align with the deeper wellsprings of life to
create for yourself the healthiest, happiest life you can.
The last imagery experience I will share with you is the
development of an image of greater wellness. As with
all your imagery, there is no right or wrong image to
have. You will find it valuable, however, to create for
yourself an image of what you believe you can become.
This image may serve as a blueprint or goal to work
toward, or may serve as an affirmation of the health and
well-being you already experience.

As usual, make yourself comfortable and arrange
not to be disturbed for approximately twenty minutes.

SCRIPT:

Image of Wellness

Begin as usual by taking a comfortable position
and loosening any restrictive clothing or jewelry . . .

take a couple of deep, full breaths and let the out breath
be a real "letting go" kind of breath . . . imagine that
with each exhalation you begin to release and relax any
unnecessary tension you feel. . . .

Allow your breathing to take its natural rate and
rhythm . . . allow yourself to relax more deeply with
each breath . . . allow the gentle movement of your
chest and abdomen to take you more deeply inside . . .
invite your body to relax and become comfortably
supported by the surface beneath it. . . .

As you relax more deeply, your mind can become
quiet and still . . . when you are ready, imagine yourself going inside to that special inner place of deep
peacefulness and concentration you have visited before
. . . take some time to notice what you see there today
. . . what you hear in this special place . . . any aroma
or fragrance that is there . . . and especially the sense of
peacefulness, quiet, and security that you feel in this
place. . . .

This is your special inner place . . . a place you can
come to for rest . . . for healing . . . for learning things
that will be helpful to you. . . .

Take some time and find the spot where you feel
most deeply relaxed, most quiet, centered, and connected to the natural healing qualities of this special
place. . . . allow yourself to sense the healing qualities
of this place supporting and nourishing your vitality
and movement toward greater wellness. . . .

When you are ready, allow an image of you enjoying wellness to arise . . . welcome the image as it
forms in your awareness, and allow it to become clear
. . . take some time to notice what you observe . . . it
may look like you or be a symbolic representation . . .
what does it look like? . . . What is it wearing, if

anything? . . . How does it move, and how does it hold itself? . . . What is its face like? . . .

How does the image seem to feel? . . . Notice what this image is doing . . . are there other people, places, or things in this image of wellness? . . .

What are the qualities this image embodies? . . . What is it about this image that conveys a sense of wellness to you? . . . Are there particular qualities that seem to be intimately connected with its wellness? . . .

When you feel ready, imagine yourself becoming the image . . . notice how that feels . . . notice your posture, your face . . . especially notice the feelings of well-being you experience. . . .

Imagine looking out of the eyes of the image . . . how does the world look from here? . . . What is your world view? . . . If you had a motto, what would it be? . . .

Imagine looking back at yourself . . . how do you look from this perspective? . . . What do you think of this person you are looking at? . . . How do you feel about this person? . . . Is there anything you know that would be helpful for this person to know? . . .

Become yourself again, and continue to feel the qualities and feelings of wellness within you . . . observe the image of wellness once more . . . does it seem different in any way? . . . Is there anything you understand about it now that you didn't before? . . .

Is there anything that stands in the way of your moving more toward that experience of wellness in your daily life? . . .

What issues or concerns arise as you consider this? . . . How might you deal with them in a healthy way and take a step toward greater wellness today? . . .

When you are ready, slowly return to your waking consciousness, remembering what has been important to you in this experience . . . when you come fully awake, take some time to write about your experience. . . .

Evaluating Your Experience

What was your image of wellness? How did it feel to see and then become that image? Do you think it's possible for you to be like this image?

What was it about the image that made it ideal? What were the qualities it had that represented wellness? Could you sense them, even potentially, in yourself? Can you now?

What stands in the way of your manifesting more of this wellness in your everyday life? How do you think you might begin to deal with these obstacles constructively?

What else was important to you in this experience?

Discrimination and The Wellness Image

Be sure to focus on the qualities of wellness in your image. A potential trap in wellness imagery is creating a model image that you cannot possibly match. Bill, a fifty-seven-year-old mechanic who had been depressed for months, imagined Joe Montana, the San Francisco Forty-Niners quarterback, as his wellness image. I asked him to describe what was attractive to him about this image, and he responded, "He's young, handsome, rich, and successful. And all the girls like him." Bill was none of these things. As a matter of fact, he was overweight, ordinary looking, pressed for cash, and barely tolerated by his wife of thirty years. As he compared himself to his image of Joe Montana, he began to feel even more depressed. Then I asked him to tell me if there were any personal qualities he admired in Joe Montana, and after a short while he answered, "Yeah, he knows his job, comes through in the clutch, and his teammates know they can depend on him." As he thought about these qualities, Bill realized that he, too, had similar qualities, but had not been valuing them sufficiently. He recounted many times that co-workers and family members had come to him for help and how he had always responded positively and gener-ously. He said he was the kind of guy that people felt they could depend on, and he had always done his work carefully and with integrity. This session was the begin-ning of an upward mood swing for Bill, as he began to acknowledge and affirm his own accomplishments and self-worth.

The lesson here is not to focus on external posses-sions or looks in the wellness image, but on qualities and attitudes. Your wellness image should inspire you, not depress you. It should give you a vision of what you could be.

Another important evaluation to make of your wellness image is whether it is a meaningful, desirable image for you. Make sure it is not the image your parents have for you, or the image the latest fashion magazine has of wellness. Work with your imagery until you have an image that is attractive and achievable for you, and use it as a blueprint for your movement toward higher-level wellness.

As you write about your experiences, you may become aware of other aspects of wellness that you value. If there are obstacles in the path of your movement toward this ideal state, you might want to consult your inner advisor about healthy ways to work with them. If you notice any reluctance to moving toward this well state, look for a part of you that may have some concerns about it, and listen to its objections. Look for ways to honor its concerns, yet continue your journey upward toward a fuller and healthier experience of life.

As you enjoy more wellness, your goals and imagery may change to include aspects and qualities you cannot now imagine. Healing, growth, and life are continuous and constantly changing. Used with skill and respect, your imagination can be a valuable navigational tool in life. It can help you take your bearings and set your sights on the healthiest, happiest life you can imagine. Use it often, use it well, and use it to make the world a better place.

Appendix A: Using Imagery for Specific Health Problems

Imagery treats people, not diseases. Nevertheless, you may want to know how it can be used in some of the common conditions listed below.

While imagery does not always lead to cure, it is almost always helpful in reducing the severity or frequency of symptoms, improving your relationship with an illness, and helping you develop greater peace of mind whatever your physical condition.

Appropriate medical attention is assumed in all cases.

The process for working with any illness is basically the same. Begin with BASIC RELAXATION SKILLS and DEEPENING TECHNIQUES to reduce stress, and prepare yourself for working with HEALING IMAGERY. The specific healing imagery you create will naturally vary with your perception of your illness and its potential healing.

Use your INNER ADVISOR and LISTENING TO YOUR SYMPTOMS to develop more awareness about the nature of the illness, its meaning for you, and any needs that it fills. Then use them to find healthier ways to fill the same needs, and use TURNING INSIGHT INTO ACTION to make necessary changes.

Use the WELLNESS IMAGERY to further motivate and affirm your healing, and be aware of RESISTANCE if you find yourself stopping your work for any reason.

Examples follow for some specific conditions.

I. STRESS REDUCTION (See Chapters One, Four, Seven, and Nine for case histories)

1) Learn BASIC RELAXATION SKILLS, and practice twice a day until you learn to relax. This usually takes between three and seven days.
2) Then learn DEEPENING SKILLS, and practice them regularly.
3) Use your INNER ADVISOR to help you identify sources of your stress and find healthy ways of reacting to them.
4) Use LISTENING TO YOUR SYMPTOMS to gain a deeper understanding of stress-related symptoms, whether physical, emotional, or behavioral.
5) Use TURNING INSIGHT INTO ACTION to help you make changes in your attitudes or actions that will reduce your stress level and its manifestations.
6) Use WELLNESS IMAGERY to create a vision of an attainable but less stressful and happier lifestyle for you.

II. PAIN RELIEF (See Chapters Four, Five, Six, Seven, and Nine for case histories)

1) Learn BASIC RELAXATION SKILLS and DEEPENING TECHNIQUES and use them often. Relaxation alone may reduce the intensity or severity of your pain.

2) Use HEALING IMAGERY to imagine the pain and its resolution in the deeply relaxed state. Practice frequently, experimenting with different images until you can change the pain sensations.

3) Use your INNER ADVISOR and LISTENING TO YOUR SYMPTOMS to understand the nature of your pain and to find ways to relieve it.

4) TURNING INSIGHT INTO ACTION will help you make changes indicated in your exploration with insight imagery.

5) LEARNING FROM YOUR RESISTANCE may help you identify any hidden benefit of the pain.

III. ADDICTION AND HABIT CHANGE
(Smoking, Alcohol, Drug, and Food Abuse)

1) Learn and practice BASIC RELAXATION SKILLS and DEEPENING TECHNIQUES until you can relax at will. This will begin to reduce anxiety and may relieve some or all of your cravings.

2) Use HEALING IMAGERY and WELLNESS IMAGERY to create vivid images of the benefits you will enjoy when you change your habits. The best images are the ones that have real meaning for you. Imagine yourself having already made the changes you want to make, and amplify any positive feelings you have as you imagine yourself being this way. Imagine this, and affirm the change in deep relaxation three times a day, and think of it as often as possible at other times.

3) Use your INNER ADVISOR to help you create healing imagery and guide you as you change. If you are in a twelve-step program such as Alcoholics Anonymous or Overeaters Anonymous, you will find this tech-

nique quite compatible with the eleventh step of
your program.
4) Consider your habit a symptom, and use LISTENING
   TO YOUR SYMPTOMS to understand the needs it fills
   and how you could fill those needs in healthier ways.
5) Be alert for RESISTANCE, and use the script to help
   unite all your inner parts in a movement toward
   better health.
6) TURNING INSIGHT INTO ACTION will help you anticipate obstacles to your success and prepare plans to
   deal with them in healthy ways.

IV. CANCER (See Chapters Two and Eleven for case
histories)

1) Use BASIC RELAXATION SKILLS, then DEEPENING
   TECHNIQUES to reduce anxiety and prepare yourself
   to use healing imagery.
2) Use HEALING IMAGERY to imagine your immune
   system healthy and powerful, overcoming and destroying your cancer. Include any regular medical
   treatments you may be taking in your imagery.
   Imagine them (whether radiation, chemotherapy, or
   surgery) as allies in your healing process, and imagine that your healthy cells can tolerate their effects
   and remain in good health.
3) Use your INNER ADVISOR and LISTENING TO YOUR
   SYMPTOMS to explore any function your illness may
   serve and to develop healthier ways to fulfill those
   functions.
4) Use TURNING INSIGHT INTO ACTION to help you
   make habit, nutritional, attitudinal or lifestyle
   changes that support your healing.

5) Use WELLNESS IMAGERY to vividly imagine your-self as healthy as possible, recovered, and leading a life you can enjoy.

V. ARTHRITIS (See Chapters Six and Nine for case histories)

1) Use BASIC RELAXATION SKILLS, then DEEPENING TECHNIQUES to reduce stress and muscle tension and prepare yourself to use healing imagery.
2) Use HEALING IMAGERY to create an image of your arthritis and its healing. You may want to first focus on one joint, and then compare it after a while to the others. Alternatively, you may create an image for the arthritic process in general and imagine healing throughout your body.
3) Practice deep relaxation and HEALING IMAGERY reg-ularly, at least twice a day for fifteen to twenty minutes at a time, for three weeks, then evaluate your progress.
4) Use your INNER ADVISOR and LISTENING TO YOUR SYMPTOMS scripts to explore any function your illness may serve and to develop healthier ways to meet the same objectives. Use them also to identify other ways you can support your body's natural ability to fight inflammation.
5) Use TURNING INSIGHT INTO ACTION to help you make habit, nutritional, attitudinal, or lifestyle changes that support your healing.
6) Use LEARNING FROM YOUR RESISTANCE if you become stuck for any length of time in your work.
7) Use WELLNESS IMAGERY to vividly imagine your-

self healthy, flexible, recovered, and leading a life
you can enjoy.

VI. ALLERGIES (See Chapters Four, Six, Seven and
Eleven for case histories)

1) Use BASIC RELAXATION SKILLS, then DEEPENING
   TECHNIQUES to reduce stress and prepare yourself
   to use healing imagery.
2) Use HEALING IMAGERY to create an image of your
   allergies and their healing. You may want to create
   an image of your immune cells being healthy and
   active yet calm, without any need to react to pollens,
   dust, or other harmless stimuli. Or you might imagine your mucous membranes, or other affected tissues, healthy and strong.
3) Practice deep relaxation and HEALING IMAGERY regularly, at least twice a day for fifteen to twenty
   minutes at a time, for three weeks, then evaluate
   your progress.
4) Use your INNER ADVISOR and LISTENING TO YOUR
   SYMPTOMS scripts to explore any function your
   illness may serve, and to develop healthier ways to
   meet the same objectives. Use them also to identify
   other ways you can support your body's natural
   health and balance.
5) Use TURNING INSIGHT INTO ACTION to help you
   make habit, nutritional, attitudinal, or lifestyle
   changes that support immune system function.
6) Use LEARNING FROM YOUR RESISTANCE if you
   become stuck for any length of time in your work.
7) Use WELLNESS IMAGERY to vividly imagine yourself healthy, recovered, and leading a life you can
   enjoy.

VII. ASTHMA (See Chapters Seven and Eleven for case histories)

WARNING: If you have asthma that reacts to stress or emotional situations, you are a good candidate for working with imagery. At first, however, you may unwittingly provoke an attack. *BE SURE TO HAVE MEDICATIONS THAT RELIABLY RELIEVE YOUR WHEEZING AT HAND AS YOU BEGIN TO WORK WITH IMAGERY.* Also remember that anything you bring on with imagery can usually be relieved with imagery.

1) Use BASIC RELAXATION SKILLS, then DEEPENING TECHNIQUES to reduce stress and prepare yourself to use healing imagery.
2) Use HEALING IMAGERY to create an image of your asthma and its healing. If you have trouble finding an image, you may want to use an image of breathing through open, relaxed bronchial tubes, or of calm, stable mast cells in your lungs (See Chapter Six).
3) Practice deep relaxation and HEALING IMAGERY regularly, at least twice a day for fifteen to twenty minutes at a time, for three weeks, then evaluate your progress.
4) Use your INNER ADVISOR and LISTENING TO YOUR SYMPTOMS scripts to explore any function your illness may serve and to develop healthier ways to meet the same objectives. Use them also to identify other ways you can support your body's natural health and balance.
5) Use TURNING INSIGHT INTO ACTION to help you make habit, nutritional, attitudinal, or lifestyle changes that support your healing.
6) Use LEARNING FROM YOUR RESISTANCE script if

you become stuck for any length of time in your
work.

7) Use WELLNESS IMAGERY to vividly imagine yourself healthy, breathing easily, and doing activities
you enjoy.

VIII. HEART DISEASE

WARNING: If you have angina (heart pains) or an
unstable heart condition, imagery may occasionally
bring on your symptoms. While symptoms precipitated
by imagery can almost always be relieved by imagery,
*BE SURE TO HAVE MEDICATIONS AT HAND
THAT CAN RELIABLY RELIEVE YOUR SYMP-
TOMS IF THEY SHOULD OCCUR.*

1) Use BASIC RELAXATION SKILLS, then DEEPENING
TECHNIQUES to reduce stress and prepare yourself
to use healing imagery.
2) Use HEALING IMAGERY to create an image of your
problem and its healing. If you have difficulty creating an image of your own, you may want to imagine
the blood supply to your heart being abundant and
the arteries that bring the blood being open and
flexible. You may also want to imagine the heart
muscle as strong, radiant, and healthy, easily pump-
ing oxygen rich blood to all parts of your body.
3) Practice deep relaxation and HEALING IMAGERY regularly, at least twice a day for fifteen to twenty
minutes at a time, for three weeks, then evaluate
your progress.
4) Use your INNER ADVISOR and LISTENING TO YOUR
SYMPTOMS scripts to explore any function your

illness may serve and to develop healthier ways to meet the same objectives. Use them also to identify other ways you can support your heart's natural function.

5) Use TURNING INSIGHT INTO ACTION to help you make habit, nutritional, attitudinal, or lifestyle changes that support your recovery.

6) Use LEARNING FROM YOUR RESISTANCE if you become stuck for any length of time in your work.

7) Use WELLNESS IMAGERY to vividly imagine yourself healthy, active, and leading a life full of activities you can enjoy.

IX. HIGH BLOOD PRESSURE (HYPERTENSION)

1) Use BASIC RELAXATION SKILLS, then DEEPENING TECHNIQUES to induce the relaxation response and prepare yourself to use healing imagery.

2) Use HEALING IMAGERY to create an image of your high blood pressure and its healing. If you have difficulty creating an image of your own, you may want to imagine your blood flowing easily through open, relaxed blood vessels all the way to the tips of your fingers and toes. Another alternative is to imagine your blood pressure being taken and seeing the numbers you desire on the blood pressure gauge. (Talk with your doctor or Heart Association to determine normal levels for your age.)

3) Practice deep relaxation and HEALING IMAGERY regularly, at least twice a day for fifteen to twenty minutes at a time, for three weeks, then evaluate your progress.

4) Use your INNER ADVISOR and LISTENING TO YOUR SYMPTOMS scripts to explore any function your illness may serve and to develop healthier ways to meet the same objectives. Use them also to identify other ways you can support your body's natural balance and health.

5) Use TURNING INSIGHT INTO ACTION to help you make habit, nutritional, attitudinal, or lifestyle changes that can lower your blood pressure.

6) Use LEARNING FROM YOUR RESISTANCE if you become stuck for any length of time in your work.

7) Use WELLNESS IMAGERY to vividly imagine yourself healthy, active, and relaxed, and leading a life you can enjoy.

8) If you need to take blood pressure medications, include them in your HEALING IMAGERY as allies.

X. *HEADACHES* (See Chapters Four and Six for case histories)

1) Use BASIC RELAXATION SKILLS, then DEEPENING TECHNIQUES to reduce stress, relieve muscle tension, and prepare yourself to use healing imagery.

2) Use HEALING IMAGERY to create an image of your headaches and their healing. If you have difficulty creating an image yourself, you might imagine that the pain melts and drains out the pores of your skin as you breathe, or that your forehead and scalp are cool and relaxed. You could also imagine your brain dripping pain-relieving substances into your bloodstream, and imagine them traveling directly to the site of your pain.

3) Practice deep relaxation and HEALING IMAGERY regularly, at least twice a day for fifteen to twenty

minutes at a time, for three weeks, then evaluate
your progress.

4) Use your INNER ADVISOR and LISTENING TO YOUR
SYMPTOMS scripts to explore any function your
headaches may serve and to develop healthier ways
to meet the same objectives. Use them also to identify other ways you can support your body's natural
balance and health.

5) Use TURNING INSIGHT INTO ACTION to help you
make habit, nutritional, attitudinal, or lifestyle
changes that can prevent headaches.

6) Use LEARNING FROM YOUR RESISTANCE if you
become stuck for any length of time in your work.

7) Use WELLNESS IMAGERY to vividly imagine yourself healthy, relaxed, pain-free, and leading a life
filled with activities you can enjoy.

XI. NECK AND BACK PAIN (See Chapters Five
and Six for case histories)

1) Use BASIC RELAXATION SKILLS, then DEEPENING
TECHNIQUES to reduce stress and muscle spasm and
prepare yourself to use healing imagery.

2) Use HEALING IMAGERY to create an image of your
pain and its healing. If you have difficulty creating
your own image, you may want to imagine breathing into your pain, imagining that each breath re-
leases a bit of tension and pain. Imagine your neck
and back muscles becoming very long, very wide,
and very flat as you breathe in and out of the painful
area, or imagine your brain dripping pain-relieving
hormones into your blood, and imagine them traveling directly to the site of your pain.

3) Practice deep relaxation and HEALING IMAGERY regularly, at least twice a day for fifteen to twenty minutes at a time, for three weeks, then evaluate your progress.

4) Use your INNER ADVISOR and LISTENING TO YOUR SYMPTOMS scripts to explore any function your problem may serve and to develop healthier ways to meet the same objectives. Use them also to identify other ways you can support your body's natural ability to recover from injury.

5) Use TURNING INSIGHT INTO ACTION to help you make habit, nutritional, attitudinal, or lifestyle changes that support more rapid healing.

6) Use LEARNING FROM YOUR RESISTANCE if you become stuck for any length of time in your work.

7) Use WELLNESS IMAGERY to vividly imagine yourself healthy, completely recovered, and leading a life filled with activities you enjoy.

XII. ANXIETY, DEPRESSION, INSOMNIA, AND OTHER MENTAL SYMPTOMS

1) Use BASIC RELAXATION SKILLS, then DEEPENING TECHNIQUES to reduce stress and prepare yourself to use healing imagery.

2) Use HEALING IMAGERY to create an image of your symptom and its healing. If no personal image comes, anxiety might be imagined as an electrical overload, and its relief imagined as an orderly, calm flow of energy throughout the system. Depression might be a black hole that can be filled with light, love, or people and things that give you pleasure. Insomniacs might imagine themselves sleeping safely

through the night and awakening refreshed and energetic.

3) Practice deep relaxation and HEALING IMAGERY regularly, at least twice a day for fifteen to twenty minutes at a time, for three weeks, then evaluate your progress.

4) Use your INNER ADVISOR and LISTENING TO YOUR SYMPTOMS scripts to explore any function your symptoms may serve and to develop healthier ways to meet the same objectives. Use them also to identify other ways you can support your body's natural balance and health.

5) Use TURNING INSIGHT INTO ACTION to help you make habit, nutritional, attitudinal, or lifestyle changes that support your well-being.

6) Use LEARNING FROM YOUR RESISTANCE if you become stuck for any length of time in your work.

7) Use WELLNESS IMAGERY to vividly imagine yourself healthy, calm, energetic, rested, and leading a life full of activities you enjoy.

XIII. COLDS, FLUS, RECURRENT INFECTIONS, AND IMMUNITY

1) Use BASIC RELAXATION SKILLS, then DEEPENING TECHNIQUES to reduce stress and prepare yourself to use healing imagery.

2) Use HEALING IMAGERY to create an image of your symptoms, your immune system, and your healing. If you have trouble creating a personal image, you may want to focus on certain symptoms, such as congestion, and imagine cleansing your mucous membranes with an antiseptic, decongestant solu-

tion. You may also want to imagine your immune cells as healthy, numerous, active, and effective in eliminating unwelcome virus or bacteria from your system.

3) Practice deep relaxation and HEALING IMAGERY regularly, at least twice a day for fifteen to twenty minutes at a time, for three weeks, then evaluate your progress.

4) Use your INNER ADVISOR and LISTENING TO YOUR SYMPTOMS scripts to explore any function your illness may serve and to develop healthier ways to meet the same objectives. Use the same techniques to identify other ways you can support your body's natural ability to fight infection and inflammation.

5) Use TURNING INSIGHT INTO ACTION to help you make habit, nutritional, attitudinal, or lifestyle changes that support your healing.

6) Use LEARNING FROM YOUR RESISTANCE if you become stuck for any length of time in your work.

7) Use WELLNESS IMAGERY to vividly imagine yourself healthy, fully recovered, and leading an active life you can enjoy.

Appendix B: Resource Guide

I. Books

Achterberg, Jeanne (1985), *Imagery in Healing: Shamanism and Modern Medicine*. Boston: New Science Library/Shambala.

This is a must read. Provides in-depth scientific underpinnings to the imagery techniques you have learned and a long-overlooked historical account of nonmedical healing in the Western world.

Andersen, Marianne S., and Savary, Louis M. (1972), *Passages: A Guide for Pilgrims of The Mind*. New York: Harper & Row Publishers.

Guided imagery explorations for increased awareness in many health-related areas from body tension to relationships.

Assagioli, Roberto, M.D., (1974), *The Act of Will*. Baltimore: Penguin Books, Inc.

Assagioli's thorough consideration of the will. If grounding is your "weak spot," read this.

Assagioli, Roberto, M.D., (1971), *Psychosynthesis*. New York: The Viking Press.

More a book for practitioners than the layperson, but outlines Psychosynthesis as originally conceived by its founder.

Barnard, Christiaan, (1981), *The Body Machine*. New York: Crown Publishers, Inc. New York.

Some excellent illustrations and very good descriptions of how things work in your body.

203

Benson, Herbert, M.D., (1976), *The Relaxation Response*. New York: Avon Books

Dr. Benson is a pioneering researcher of the physiology of meditation and discovered that it triggers a physiologic reflex he calls the relaxation response. His subsequent research has shown it to be effective in lowering blood pressure and a host of other psychophysiologic illnesses. A very useful introductory book for someone dealing with a stress-related condition.

Bingham, June, and Tamarkin, Norman, M.D., (1985), *The Pursuit of Health*. New York: Walker & Co.

An interesting look at the multiple factors involved in health and illness as brought together by what the authors term the "intimate connector" within each person.

Bolen, Jean Shinoda, M.D., (1979), *The Tao of Psychology*. New York: Harper & Row Publishers, Inc.

An illustrative look at synchronicity, and how the inner and outer worlds interact as seen by a Jungian analyst.

Borysenko, Joan, Ph.D. (1987) *Minding the Body, Mending the Mind* Reading, Massachusetts: Addison-Wesley.

A wonderfully clear and useful book about self-healing by the co-founder and director of the Mind/Body Clinic of the New England Deaconess Hospital. Dr. Borysenko, a microbiologist, psychologist and yoga instructor, shares her broad and deep knowledge in an eminently helpful way.

Bresler, Dr. David E., (1979), New York: *Free Yourself From Pain*. Simon and Schuster.

The best self-help book there is for people with chronic pain. Includes exercises, information, progress charts, and scripts by the founder of the UCLA Pain Clinic.

Cannon, Walter B., M.D., (1967), *The Wisdom of The Body*. New York: Norton & Company Inc.

Cannon was the eminent Harvard physiologist who coined the term "homeostasis" and described the natural mechanisms the human organism possesses for maintaining balance in the face of change.

Capra, Fritjof, (1975), *The Tao of Physics*. Berkeley: Shambala.
Illustrates the parallels in modern physics and ancient Eastern philosophy, making each more accessible.

Cousins, Norman, (1979), *Anatomy of an Illness*. New York: W. W. Norton & Co.
Articulate, provocative look at the potential for self-healing and the issues that it brings to light in our health-care system.

Davis, Martha and Eshelman, Elizabeth Robbins and McKay, Matthew, (1982), *The Relaxation & Stress Reduction Workbook*. Oakland: New Harbinger Publications.
Many good relaxation/stress reduction exercises.

Dychtwald, Ken, (1977), *Body-Mind*. New York: Jove Publications, Inc.
Another perspective on the interweaving of what we call body and what we call mind, this one through the eyes of a psychologist and Reichian therapist.

Eckstein, Gustav, (1970), *The Body Has A Head*. New York: Harper & Row Publishers.
Interesting observations of mind-body interactions by a poetic neuropsychiatrist.

Edlin, Gordon and Golanty, Eric, (1982), *Health & Wellness*. Boston: Science Books International.
This is an attractive and interesting book that covers many wellness-related topics in easily digestible forms.

Epstein, Gerald, M.D., (1981), *Waking Dream Therapy*. Human Sciences Press, Inc.
Epstein, a psychiatrist, works with imagery as a waking dream in some very interesting ways.

Fiore, Neil A., Ph.D. (1984), *The Road Back to Health: Coping With the Emotional Side of Cancer*. New York: Bantam Books, Inc.
Fiore, a psychologist and cancer survivor, works with imagery and has very helpful advice and insights for people with cancer and their families.

Frank, Jerome D., (1974), *Persuasion and Healing*. New York: Schocken Books.
   A fascinating, erudite exploration of belief systems and healing by an eminent professor of psychiatry at Johns Hopkins.

Gendlin, Eugene T., (1981), *Focusing*. New York: Bantam Books, Inc.
   The elements of focusing are the essentials of working with imagery. Gendlin believes this process of quieting, paying attention to symptoms, getting a handle on them, and waiting for a "felt sense" of change to be the basis of all therapeutic effectiveness. Highly recommended.

Goleman, Daniel, (1977), *The Varieties of The Meditative Experience*. New York: Irvington Publishers, Inc.
   Scholarly yet accessible look at different forms of meditation.

Gordon, J., and Rosenthal, R., (1984), *The Healing Partnership*. Washington, D. C.: Aurora Associates.
   Four essays that point to the need and opportunity for doctors and patients to work together toward higher-quality health care.

Haas, Elson M., M.D., (1981), *Staying Healthy with the Seasons*. Millbrae, California: Celestial Arts.
   A lovely book which brings together the traditional Chinese concepts of living in harmony with nature with practical information on a wide variety of health practices from nutrition to acupuncture to imagery.

Hutschnecker, Arnold A., M.D., (1982), *The Will to Live*. New York: Cornerstone Library.
   The Simontons make this must reading for all their cancer patients.

Jacobson, Edmund, M.D., (1962), *You Must Relax*. New York: McGraw-Hill Book Company.
   Jacobson was a pioneer in the field of relaxation therapy. His exhaustive technique is rarely used today, but abridged modifications of it are probably the most widely used relaxation techniques around.

Jaffe, Dennis T., (1980), *Healing From Within*. New York: Alfred A. Knopf, Inc.
A very well-written, highly recommended book. Provides more in-depth information about the psychological and scientific basis for imagery techniques.

Jaffe, Dennis T., and Scott, Cynthia D., (1984), *From Burnout to Balance*. New York: McGraw-Hill Book Company.
Excellent, practical workbook filled with worksheets to help you move in the direction indicated by the title.

Jampolsky, Gerald G., M.D., (1979), *Love Is Letting Go of Fear*. Millbrae, California: Celestial Art.
A very popular primer on attitudinal healing.

Jolly, Dr. Richard T., (1980), *The Color Atlas of Human Anatomy*. New York: Beekman House.
A good illustrated anatomy book.

Jung, Carl G., (1984), *Man and His Symbols*. Garden City, New York: Doubleday & Company, Inc.
The most accessible book regarding Jung's work. Illustrates how symbols relate to deeply meaningful dimensions of human life.

Kapit, Wynn, and Elson, Lawrence M., (1977), *The Anatomy Coloring Book*. New York: Harper & Row Publishers, Inc.
Outline illustrations of anatomy for coloring. Often useful for getting better acquainted with a body part.

Koestler, Arthur, (1972), *The Roots of Coincidence*. New York: Random House.
A venture into a physical explanation for the phenomenon of synchronicity.

LeShan, Lawrence, (1982), *The Mechanic and the Gardener*. New York: Holt, Rhinehart, and Winston.
A very well-written book draws out the title metaphor and looks at the relationship of medicine to healing. Many practical tips for dealing with doctors and hospitals while honoring your own healing contributions.

LeShan, Lawrence, (1977), *You Can Fight For Your Life*. New York: Jove Publications.
The first book on consciously combatting cancer by a prominent psychologist who has worked with cancer patients for decades. Must reading if your problem is cancer.

Locke, Steven E., M.D., and Colligan, Douglas, (1986), *The Healer Within: The New Medicine of Mind and Body*. New York: E. P. Dutton.
Dr. Locke explains the relationships of the nervous system to the immune and other major control systems of the body and points to their relevance for medical and self-treatment. There is a very useful resource guide included as well.

Mason, L. John, (1980), *Guide to Stress Reduction*. Culver City, California: Peace Press.
A gentle, practical guide to reducing stress.

McMahon, Carol E., (1986), *Where Medicine Fails*. New York: Conch Magazine Ltd.
McMahon, a medical historian, looks at the historical Cartesian split of body and mind and suggests a remedy that can lead to a more holistic approach to health.

Mindell, Arnold, (1985), *Working With The Dreaming Body*. Boston: Routledge & Kegan Paul.
A challenging book full of cases of healing where no differentiation is made of body, mind, dream, or symbol.

Mishlove, Jeffrey, (1975), *The Roots of Consciousness*. New York: Random House, Inc.
A review of the evolution of ideas of consciousness.

Nilsson, Lennart, (1973), *Behold Man*. Boston: Little Brown and Company.
Remarkable photographs of everything from hormone crystals to intrauterine development. A good source of images.

Ornish, Dean, M.D., (1982), *Stress, Diet, and Your Health*. New York: Holt, Rinehart and Winston.
Dr. Ornish is a leading researcher in heart disease and its prevention and treatment through natural means. Here he presents

the program that has successfully been used with heart patients and those at high risk. The program includes stretching, exercise, diet, relaxation, and imagery.

Ornstein, Robert E., (1968), *The Nature of Human Consciousness*. San Francisco: W. H. Freeman and Company.
A collection of basic readings on split-brain findings, Eastern and Western psychologies, and the psychophysiology of consciousness as understood in the mid-sixties. To some, this will be old hat; to many, it will still be new information.

Ornstein, Robert E., (1977), *The Psychology of Consciousness*. New York: Harcourt Brace Jovanovich, Inc.
A psychology text integrating Eastern psychologies, meditative, intuitive, and self-regulatory capacities into a model of consciousness that includes but extends classical Western psychology. Partly technical but accessible to the interested layperson.

Ornstein, Robert E., and Thompson, Richard F., (1984), *The Amazing Brain*. Boston: Houghton Mifflin Company.
Fascinating tour through the evolution and function of the brain and mind. Thought-provoking and illuminating illustrations well worth a look.

Oyle, Irving, (1979), *The New American Medicine Show*. Santa Cruz, California: Unity Press.

Oyle, Irving, (1974), *The Healing Mind*. Millbrae, California: Celestial Arts.
All of Dr. Oyle's books are provocative and illuminating and well worth reading. These are the two most easily available.

Pelletier, Kenneth R., (1979), *Holistic Medicine*. New York: Delacorte Press/Seymour Lawrence.
As always with Pelletier's books, this one is authoritative and well-researched. Makes a very coherent argument for making holism an integral part of medicine.

Pelletier, Kenneth R., (1977), *Mind as Healer Mind as Slayer*. New York: Dell Publishing Company.
Classic, well-documented review of mind-body interactions in health as of mid-1970s.

Pelletier, Kenneth R., and Garfield, Charles, (1976), *Consciousness East and West*. New York: Harper & Row Publishers.
Compares Eastern and Western psychologies and their paradigms of consciousness.

Popenoe, Cris, (1979), *Inner Development*. Washington, D.C.: Yes! Inc.
A rich annotated resource guide for the inner explorer.

Porter, Garrett, and Norris, Patricia A. (1985), *Why Me: Harnessing The Healing Power of The Human Spirit*. Walpole, New Hampshire: Stillpoint.
Dr. Norris is a psychologist at the Menninger Foundation who worked with Garrett, a nine-year-old boy with an inoperable terminal brain tumor. They worked together with imagery and visualization techniques and Garrett's tumor disappeared. Both inspirational and instructive for anyone working with imagery.

Progoff, Ira, (1975), *At A Journal Workshop*. New York: Dialogue House Library.
Progoff, a depth psychologist, teaches a very helpful way of using a journal to gain psychological understanding and explains it thoroughly in this book.

Remen, Naomi, M.D., (1980), *The Human Patient*. Garden City, New York: Anchor Press/Doubleday.
An inspiring book that illustrates how modern medicine can be practiced with respect for the human dimensions of healing. Filled with touching, powerful case histories and clear models for practice.

Ryan, Regina Sara and Travis, John W., M.D., (1981), *Wellness Workbook*. Berkeley: Ten Speed Press.
Extremely useful guidebook to exploring the many dimensions of wellness and health. Highly recommended.

Samuels, Mike, M.D., and Bennett, Hal, (1978), *The Well Body Book*. New York: Random House.
A classic in self-care, this book contains many practical tips for taking care of yourself naturally. Introduces many simple relaxation and imagery techniques as well.

Samuels, Mike, M.D., and Samuels, Nancy, (1975), *Seeing With The Mind's Eye*. New York: Random House, Inc.
Classic overview of the history and current uses of imagery. Contains many scripts and suggestions for using imagery for healing and in daily life, as well as interesting photographs and illustrations. Highly recommended.

Selye, Hans, M.D., (1956), *The Stress of Life*. New York: McGraw-Hill Company.
Selye's original classic describes the development of the stress concept, his early research, and suggestions for living with stress.

Shames, Richard, M.D., and Sterin, Chuck, (1978), *Healing With Mind Power*. Emmaus, Pennsylvania: Rodale Press.
Useful book by a prominent holistic physician and a psychologist teaches self-hypnosis techniques for dealing with common health problems.

Siegel, Bernard, M.D., (1986), *Love, Medicine, and Miracles*. New York: Harper & Row.
Dr. Siegel is a cancer surgeon at Yale and an enthusiastic believer in the importance of emotions and will to live in recovering from cancer. His anecdotes about the exceptional cancer patients he has worked with are inspirational and will be supportive of anyone who wants to use these methods to help himself heal.

Simeons, A.T.W., M.D., (1960), *Man's Presumptuous Brain*. New York: E. P. Dutton & Company, Inc.
An entertaining, informative look at physiology and how we consciously or unconsciously interfere with it.

Smith, Adam, (1975), *Powers of Mind*. New York: Ballantine Books.
Interesting journey through the eyes of a businessman as he explores various dimensions of the "consciousness explosion" of the early 1970s.

Volen, Michael, M.D., (1986), *In Search of Health*. Mill Valley, California: Gateway Press.
Sensible, readable book looks at alternative medicine, conventional medicine, and self-care and their relationships in health care.

II. *Tapes*

There are a wide variety of tapes available that utilize guided imagery, self-hypnosis, and subliminal suggestions for healing. I am including only those resources that I have personally worked with and recommend.

Insight Publishing, P.O. Box 1933, Mill Valley, CA 94942

This is my company. We publish tapes of all the scripts in this book, as well as lecture tapes on imagery, self-healing, and related topics by prominent authorities in the field. Send for free catalogue.

Steven Halpern Tapes, 1775 Old Country Road, #10, Belmont, CA 94002

Dr. Halpern has been called the "Mozart of the New Age." He has a wide selection of relaxing music tapes, both with and without subliminal suggestions for everything from pain relief to improved memory. Send for free catalogue.

The Source: Emmet Miller, M.D., Emmet Miller Tapes, 945 Evelyn Street, Menlo Park, CA 94025

Dr. Miller, a psychiatrist, hypnotist, and musician, has a very high-quality line of tapes for relaxation, pain relief, surgery preparation, habit change, and healing. Some with music, others without. Send for catalogue.

Institute for The Advancement of Human Behavior, P.O. Box 7226, Stanford, CA 94305

IAHB carries a wide variety of tapes, including imagery tapes for laypeople and professionals. Many lecture tapes from their first-rate conferences on timely health-related issues. Send for catalogue.

Medical Self-Care Catalog, P.O. Box 999, Point Reyes, CA 94956

Published by *Medical Self-Care Magazine*. They carry a variety of self-care tapes as well as other well-selected self-care items.

ISHK Book Service, P.O. Box 1062, Cambridge, MA 02238

The Institute for the Study of Human Knowledge has held some seminal conferences on the brain, the mind, and healing.

They offer a variety of both lecture and instructional tapes, many of them imagery related. Send for catalogue.

Summerset Associates, 2901 Wilshire Blvd., Suite 345, Santa Monica, CA 90403

Dr. David Bresler has an extensive catalogue of excellent tapes for both professionals and laypeople. Many of them utilize relaxation and guided imagery processes. Send for catalogue.

III. Practitioners and Centers

My office maintains a listing of health professionals who work with guided imagery around the country. If you would like a referral, please send a postcard that includes your full return address and any large cities reasonably accessible to you. We will do our best to reply within a few days. (P.O. Box 1933, Mill Valley, CA 94942.)

Index

Healing Yourself Tape Series

Dr. Rossman has professionally recorded all of the guided imagery exercises in this book. These are available as a six-cassette series that includes an explanation of how to best use the tapes and a lecture entitled "The Uses of Imagery in Medical Self-Care," given by Dr. Rossman at a national symposium on imagery and health.

The cassettes are available individually at $12.95 each or as the complete HEALING YOURSELF TAPE SERIES in vinyl binder for $59.95.

The HEALING YOURSELF TAPE SERIES includes:

#101		The Uses of Imagery in Medical Self Care
#102	Side A:	Imagery, the Tapes and Healing
	Side B:	A First Exploration in Imagery
#103	Side A:	Basic Relaxation Skills
	Side B:	Going Deeper Within
#104	Side A:	Your Healing Imagery
	Side B:	Meeting Your Inner Adviser
#105	Side A:	Listening to your Symptoms
	Side B:	Turning Insight into Action
#106	Side A:	Learning from Your Resistance
	Side B:	Your Image of Wellness

Send check or money order to:
Academy for Guided Imagery
P. O. Box 2070
Mill Valley, CA 94942

Or order by phone with VISA or MasterCard:
(415) 389-9324 or (800) 726-2070

Please include $7.00 postage and handling for complete series; $2.00 for each cassette ordered individually. California residents add sales tax. Prices subject to change.

If you are a health professional and would like information on Professional Training and Certification in Interactive Guided Imagery ℠ please contact the Academy for Guided Imagery at (800) 726-2070.